An Apostle's Life:
Conflicts Without and Fears Within

The Message of 2 Corinthians

Loren VanGalder

Spiritual Father Publications

All scripture quotations, unless otherwise indicated, are taken from the *Holy Bible*, New International Version®, NIV®. Copyright ©1973, 1978, 1984, 2011 by Biblica, Inc.™All rights reserved worldwide. The "NIV" and "New International Version" are trademarks registered in the United States Patent and Trademark Office by Biblica, Inc.™

Scripture quotations marked Amplified (AMP) are from the *Amplified New Testament*. Copyright ©1954, 1958, 1987 by the Lockman Foundation. Used by Permission of Zondervan Publishing House. All rights reserved.

Scripture quotations marked New Living Translation (NLT) are from the *Holy Bible*, New Living Translation, copyright © 1996. Used by permission of Tyndale House Publishers, Inc., Wheaton, Illinois 60189. All rights reserved.

Copyright © 2016 by Loren VanGalder. All rights reserved.

ISBN-10: 0-9897472-8-X
ISBN-13: 978-0-9897472-8-8

Table of Contents

Dedication 1

Introduction 3

Chapter 1 The Purpose of Suffering 7

    2 Corinthians 1:3-11 7

Chapter 2 Security in the Midst of Suffering 13

    2 Corinthians 1:12-24 13

Chapter 3 Love Hurts 21

    2 Corinthians 2:1-4 21

Chapter 4 Insights into Church Discipline 25

    2 Corinthians 2:5-11 25

Chapter 5 Insights into the Ministry 29

    2 Corinthians 2:12-17 29

Chapter 6 Ever-increasing Glory 33

    2 Corinthians 3 33

Chapter 7 We do not Lose Heart 39

    2 Corinthians 4 39

Chapter 8   Are You Ready for Something Totally Different? 47

    2 Corinthians 5:1-10 47

Chapter 9   The Ministry of Reconciliation 53

    2 Corinthians 5:9-21 53

Chapter 10 Receiving God's Grace in Vain 61

    2 Corinthians 6:1-2 61

Chapter 11 The Ups and Downs of Serving Christ	65
2 Corinthians 6:3-11	65
Chapter 12 We are the Temple of the Living God	71
2 Corinthians 6:14-7:1	71
Chapter 13 The Value of Relationships	81
2 Corinthians 7:2-7	81
Chapter 14 Regrets	87
2 Corinthians 7:8-16	87
Chapter 15 Generous Giving	93
2 Corinthians 8:1-24	93
Chapter 16 Freedom from Shame	107
2 Corinthians 9:1-4	107
Chapter 17 Sowing and Reaping	113
2 Corinthians 9:5-15	113
Chapter 18 Weapons for the Battle	119
2 Corinthians 10:1-6	119
Chapter 19 The Lord's Work in the Lord's Way	129
2 Corinthians 10:7-18	129
Chapter 20 The Masquerade	137
2 Corinthians 11:1-15	137
Chapter 21 Real Boasting	147

2 Corinthians 11:16-33 147
Chapter 22 Strength in Weakness 155
2 Corinthians 12:1-10 155
Chapter 23 True Apostolic Ministry 163
2 Corinthians 12:11-21 163
Chapter 24 Examine Yourself 169
2 Corinthians 13:1-6 169
Chapter 25 What is Truly Important 177
2 Corinthians 13:7-14 177
Conclusion 183
Appendix: A Biblical Understanding of
Comfort 187

Dedication

There is much talk in the church today about apostles. There is also much confusion. This book is dedicated to those men God is calling and raising up to truly be his apostles.

I would also like to thank my sister, Dr. Karen VanGalder, for her great help editing this manuscript. She has worked in the church most of her life, and has seen much of the good and the bad about church first hand!

Introduction

For many years I saw 2 Corinthians as a poor companion to Paul's content-laden first letter. I struggled with Paul's defensive tone, his "boasting," and the emphasis on the offering he was collecting. Suddenly, after almost 40 years of essentially ignoring it, I read the letter again and saw it with new eyes. God can make Scripture come alive! This letter is amazing! And there's much that's relevant to today's church, especially for leaders.

As I shared some studies on my blog I found that many people had never studied this book. Amazingly, they regularly quoted these well-known verses, but had no idea what the rest of the letter was about.

- *Now the Lord is the Spirit, and where the Spirit of the Lord is, there is freedom.* (3:17)
- *But we have this treasure in jars of clay to show that this all-surpassing power is from God and not from us.* (4:7)
- *Therefore, if anyone is in Christ, the new creation has come: The old has gone, the new is here!* (5:17)
- *We are therefore Christ's ambassadors, as though God were making his appeal through us. We implore you on Christ's behalf: Be reconciled to God. God made him who had no sin to be sin for us, so that in him we might become the righteousness of God.* (5:20-21)
- *Do not be yoked together with unbelievers.* (6:14)

- *Remember this: Whoever sows sparingly will also reap sparingly, and whoever sows generously will also reap generously. Each of you should give what you have decided in your heart to give, not reluctantly or under compulsion, for God loves a cheerful giver.* (9:6-7)

You're probably familiar with these verses as well. Do you know the context? The title I gave this book reflects what I feel is a significant theme. From all appearances, Paul's life was anything but trouble-free and victorious. He was plagued with inner struggles so intense he felt the sentence of death. If it wasn't attacks from jealous members of his own religious background he was fighting with false apostles in the church. He was in anguish over the possibility of losing a church he loved so much. There's much talk today about apostles. The gospel of success, happiness, and prosperity is heard everywhere. This letter may give you a very different view of Christianity than what you've been used to.

I think you'll be as excited about 2 Corinthians as I was while writing about. This study isn't a commentary, but is intended to clarify the message and help you apply it your life. Read it prayerfully to digest it and reflect on the issues raised.

Let's start with a look at Paul's introduction.

Chosen by God

[1]*This letter is from Paul, chosen by the will of God to be an apostle of Christ Jesus, and from our brother Timothy.*

Would Paul have chosen this career if he had known it would involve so much suffering? He didn't have a choice. It was God's choice. God chose him. God literally knocked Paul to the ground and never asked if he wanted the assignment or not (Acts 9:3-5) . This was God's will for his life, and Paul was wise enough not to fight it. God had said *"it's hard to kick against the goads"* when he called him (Acts 9:5 and 26:14). Paul had his fill of fighting God. Though an apostle's life was hard, there is no indication that Paul regretted his ministry. After all, what a privilege to be sent by God himself as a representative of Jesus Christ!

Part of the Body of Christ

One of the themes in this letter is the importance of relationships. We are part of a body, and Paul exemplified that by always having others around him. Timothy was a brother in Christ, but also Paul's beloved son in the faith.

I am writing to God's church in Corinth and to all of his holy people throughout Greece.

The letter is directed to the church in Corinth, and at many points the connections with Paul's first letter are evident. But there's also much universal truth here that Paul wanted to have shared throughout Greece.

It is God's church –not Paul's or any other apostle's – and that will be a theme in the letter, along with God's call to holiness.

[2] *May God our Father and the Lord Jesus Christ give you grace and peace.* (NLT)

Could you use some grace and peace in your life? They are gifts from God. You cannot earn them, and they are not based on your merit. I pray God would give you his grace and peace as you study this great letter.

Chapter 1 The Purpose of Suffering
2 Corinthians 1:3-11

Suffering is part of the universal human experience. We struggle to understand and escape it. Some claim that "Christ suffered, so we don't have to." But God never promises us freedom from suffering. He does, however, enter into our suffering. He is the God of all comfort.

Paul had plenty of opportunities to be comforted, since he endured great suffering. Unfortunately, while suffering is universal, finding comfort in the midst of it is not. Paul starts his letter by teaching us how to receive and give comfort. The word "comfort" appears nine times in just five verses!

³Praise be to the God and Father of our Lord Jesus Christ, the Father of compassion and the God of all comfort, ⁴ who comforts us in all our troubles, so that we can comfort those in any trouble with the comfort we ourselves receive from God. ⁵ For just as we share abundantly in the sufferings of Christ, so also our comfort abounds through Christ. ⁶ If we are distressed, it is for your comfort and salvation; if we are comforted, it is for your comfort, which produces in you patient endurance of the same sufferings we suffer. ⁷And our hope for you is firm, because we know that just as you share in our sufferings, so also you share in our comfort.

Comfort implies suffering

If everything is going great there is no need for comfort. If you want overflowing comfort, you will have overflowing suffering: *the more we suffer for Christ, the more God will shower us with his comfort through Christ* (verse 5, NLT). Paul saw sharing in Christ's suffering as a great privilege: *I want to know Christ and the power of His resurrection and the fellowship of His sufferings, becoming like him in his death* (Philippians 3:10). Is that the longing of your heart? Do you welcome suffering so you can become more Christ-like? The tremendous comfort we receive in the midst of intense suffering brings a depth in our relationship to Jesus which those who rarely suffer may never know.

Why does God allow suffering?

- He is the God of all comfort. We become more God-like as we receive comfort and share it. We especially enjoy a deeper experience of the Holy Spirit, the Comforter. And we become more compassionate, since compassion is related to comfort.

- God comforts us – but then expects us to comfort others. The more you give comfort the more the Comforter flows through you, and the more comfort you receive! To be comforted you have to be in some kind of trouble. If your life is always trouble-free you have no need of comfort. You will lack compassion and intimacy with God, and will be unable to comfort others. If you have known people who always seem to have it easy, you may be aware of how hard it is for them to minister genuine comfort. If you receive comfort but fail to pass it on, you quench the Spirit's work in your life.

- Comfort produces patient endurance. You can put up with a lot more if you know you are not alone. Someone is with you in the trial. The suffering is far worse if you are alone and never get comforted. It makes sense that a pastor or leader will experience more suffering, so they will be better equipped to comfort others.

The Bible is full of teaching on comfort. You'll find an in-depth study in the appendix, on page.

Paul's overflowing suffering

[8] We do not want you to be uninformed, brothers and sisters, about the troubles we experienced in the province of Asia. We were under great pressure, far beyond our ability to endure, so that we despaired of life itself. [9] Indeed, we felt we had received the sentence of death.

That is intense! This is Paul, the great apostle and man of faith! Have you ever despaired of life itself? When things got so bad it seemed you had received a death sentence? If not physical death, you may have experienced the death of a dream, or a relationship. There are many kinds of suffering - and they are all painful!

Paul's transparency is impressive, especially with a church that questions his leadership. Some might look at what he is going through and run the other way, thinking he was a poor example of faith and victory. Indeed, the leader needs to be careful of how much he shares about his personal life. If a church gets the sense that the pastor is falling apart and doubting God, it can devastate the whole body. On the other hand, the church needs to know that pastors are human, and go through trials like anyone else. There can be tremendous pressure on any Christian to maintain a façade of victory, which encourages artificiality.

Why would God allow such intense suffering for his chosen servant?

⁹ But this happened that we might not rely on ourselves but on God, who raises the dead.

Americans pride themselves on being self-reliant. That makes it much harder to be a Christian, since to grow in Christ we need to give up our self-reliance and rely totally on God. He will allow whatever trials are necessary to get you to a point where you have no choice but to rely on him. Even Paul still needed to learn that lesson! The more gifted and capable you are, the more suffering it takes to get you to that point. Perhaps if we consciously give up our self-reliance and allow God to take over we can avoid some of the suffering. What trials are you experiencing right now? Is it possible God is forcing you to rely on him?

And if we die in the process? No problem, since God raises the dead! Don't despair, even when you feel the sentence of death in your life, because God is able to give new life to whatever may have died!

Chapter 1 The Purpose of Suffering

How you, the church, and God all work together

[10] He has delivered us from such a deadly peril, and he will deliver us again. On him we have set our hope that he will continue to deliver us, [11] as you help us by your prayers.

- **God** doesn't spare you from deadly peril, but he does deliver you from it. He is faithful, and just as he has delivered you in the past, he will deliver you in the future. At times deliverance may mean death; taking you out of this world so you can be with him.

- **You** must hold onto hope. Keep your eyes on God in the trial and put your hope in him, based on his past faithfulness. You may be tempted to put your hope in other people, money, or your own ingenuity, but they will all fail you at some point.

- **The church** must pray. Paul acknowledged his need for their prayers. God has designed us to need each other as fellow members of his body. The Amplified version says *"While you also cooperate by your prayers for us – helping and laboring together with us."* Do you faithfully pray for others who are suffering? From the comfort of your home you can have a significant impact on suffering brothers and sisters in other parts of the world. And, amazing as it sounds, they would like to know what you are struggling with, so they can pray for you! The toughest circumstances often produce the most faithful prayer warriors! If you never let anyone know what you're going through, they can't pray for you or comfort you. If you tell someone you will pray for them, make sure you do. If you say you will pray for someone going for an important doctor's appointment in a couple of days, send them a text or Email that morning, letting them know you are praying for them. Find ways to keep abreast of suffering believers around the world. Pray for them and try to communicate with them.

[11] Then many will give thanks on our behalf for the gracious favor granted us in answer to the prayers of many.

There is one more benefit from our prayers: God receives thanksgiving and praise for the outpouring of his gracious favor. That's why it's so important to update people on answered prayers, and find out how God has helped others. Then thank him for his gracious provision.

Can you see the many ways God works through our suffering? It may not make it easier when you're despairing of life, but that's when we can receive comfort from others and experience God's deliverance. It allows others the joy and blessing of comforting us, praying, and seeing answered prayer.

God wants his comfort to overflow into your life right now. No matter how desperate your situation, he is at your side. You are not alone. Receive his comfort and thank him for his faithfulness.

Chapter 2 Security in the Midst of Suffering

2 Corinthians 1:12-24

^{12} We can say with confidence and a clear conscience that we have lived with a God-given holiness and sincerity in all our dealings. We have depended on God's grace, not on our own human wisdom. That is how we have conducted ourselves before the world, and especially toward you. (NLT)

Our conduct should be the same in the world, at church, and at home. The aim is consistency. It's easy to maintain a double standard:

- Giving less than your best at church while acting with utmost integrity at work.
- The model Christian at church who cheats on taxes or steals from the job.
- A respected man in the community who is abusive at home.

It's tremendously freeing to maintain a clear conscience in all your relationships! Strive to act with integrity, holiness, pure motives, and godly sincerity, so you can hold your head high on the job, before the Lord, and with your family. That requires God's grace. On your own you'll find it nearly impossible to conduct yourself in such an upright manner. Far from proudly boasting about his conduct, Paul confesses that even he needed that grace! If we don't rely on God's grace, the temptation is to rely on the worldly wisdom James wrote about:

> *Who is wise and understanding among you? Let them show it by their good life, by deeds done in the humility that comes from wisdom. But if you harbor bitter envy and selfish ambition in your hearts, do not boast about it or deny the truth. Such "wisdom" does not come down from heaven but is earthly, unspiritual, demonic. For where you have envy and selfish ambition, there you find disorder and every evil practice* (James 3:13-16).

Paul may be suggesting that the false apostles in Corinth, in their self-promotion and self-centeredness, were acting with this worldly wisdom.

[13] *For we do not write you anything you cannot read or understand. And I hope that,* [14] *as you have understood us in part, you will come to understand fully that you can boast of us just as we will boast of you in the day of the Lord Jesus.*

Not everyone would agree that Paul always wrote so clearly. It was probably one of his detractors' accusations. Peter wrote about him: *His letters contain some things that are hard to understand, which ignorant and unstable people distort, as they do the other Scriptures, to their own destruction* (2 Peter 3:16).

Paul probably knew he wasn't always easy to understand. He didn't intend to write above their heads, but 2000 years later some of his writings still puzzle us! Whether it's Scripture or inspired preaching, it's common to understand in part. Gradually we come to understand more, but we will only fully understand when we're with the Lord (1 Corinthians 13:12).

Verse fourteen offers a beautiful picture of believers standing before Jesus, boasting of pastors who had faithfully ministered the Word. At the same time those ministers boast of their faithful disciples! Can you think of someone who will be boasting about you? Is there anyone you will boast about when you stand before the Lord?

Was Paul unreliable?

15 Because I was confident of this, I wanted to visit you first so that you might benefit twice. 16 I wanted to visit you on my way to Macedonia and to come back to you from Macedonia, and then to have you send me on my way to Judea. 17 Was I fickle when I intended to do this? Or do I make my plans in a worldly manner so that in the same breath I say both "Yes, yes" and "No, no"?

When he failed to make a promised visit, Paul's detractors promptly labeled him unreliable. He was accused of:

- Being fickle; not praying or seriously thinking about what he was doing.

- Making plans in a worldly manner with flawed human reasoning, instead of being guided by the Holy Spirit.

- Being purposely misleading, saying "yes" and "no" in the same breath or saying "yes" with no intention of doing it. In some cultures that's done to avoid offending someone. Or it may just be easier to say yes. Christians can easily fall into the same habit, but we must be honest and true to our word.

The Corinthians should have known that all Paul's plans were subject to God's will. The closing of his first letter (1 Corinthians 16:5-9) included words like *"perhaps," "I hope,"* and *"if the Lord permits."*

[18] As surely as God is faithful, our word to you does not waver between "Yes" and "No." [19] For Jesus Christ, the Son of God, does not waver between "Yes" and "No." He is the one whom Silas, Timothy, and I preached to you, and as God's ultimate "Yes," he always does what he says. [20] For all of God's promises have been fulfilled in Christ with a resounding "Yes!" And through Christ, our "Amen" (which means "Yes") ascends to God for his glory.

In Christ everything is yes!

If the Corinthians feel that Paul is unreliable, then Paul is concerned that his message might also be questioned. His detractors tried to exploit that, but Paul assures them that Jesus and his Word are unchanging.

This letter started on a heavy note. Suffering can cause us to lose focus, but now Paul calls us to stay unwaveringly on message, not getting distracted by all the possible side issues. Be positive and affirmative: In Christ all God's promises – indeed, everything – is "Yes!"

Chapter 2 Security in the Midst of Suffering

Paul has raised some difficult issues in this first chapter. He concludes by pointing to ways that God, you, and believers in the church can respond to these challenges.

God: Amazing security in the midst of suffering

[21] Now it is God who makes both us and you stand firm in Christ. He anointed us, [22] set his seal of ownership on us, and put his Spirit in our hearts as a deposit, guaranteeing what is to come.

- He *makes* you stand firm in Christ. It's not up to you! You definitely have your part to play, but God does everything in his unlimited power to make sure you stand firm. If you are feeling shaky, perhaps you're trying too hard to stand in your own strength.

- He anointed you when you were saved and filled with the Holy Spirit. Do you sense that anointing? Do you need a fresh anointing?

- He set a seal of ownership on you, like a brand on cattle. Remind Satan of that when he tries to tell you that God doesn't care about you!

- He put his Spirit in your heart as a deposit. The Greek word conveys the certainty that since you have the initial deposit, you can be assured of everything promised you. It's common to say there are no guarantees in life, but what better guarantee do you want than this!

You: Know your limits

²³ I call God as my witness—and I stake my life on it—that it was in order to spare you that I did not return to Corinth.

Sometimes it is wise to stay away! Paul knew a visit at that time would be unproductive. It was not a decision made lightly. He truly wanted to go, but out of love for them he chose to spare them from what would have been another painful visit. What is striking is his fervor in defending the truth of what he's saying – he calls God as witness, and stakes his very life on it!

The church: Helping you stand firm by faith

²⁴ Not that we lord it over your faith, but we work with you for your joy, because it is by faith you stand firm.

The church plays an important role in sustaining believers through difficult times, primarily by encouraging their faith. Leaders that lord it over the flock can discourage faith. Instead, we should all work together for a common goal. Paul's relationship with the Corinthians had become burdensome and difficult. It should have been joyful, and Paul hopes it will be once again.

The Corinthians must stand firm in their faith, or they will not survive. We see here the endless tension between God's sovereignty and our responsibility. Paul just said God *makes us* stand firm – now he says it is *by faith* that we stand firm. Which is it? Both! God does his part, but faith - belief in God and what he has said and done – is necessary on our part. In the same way, God paid the price for your sin — but you must accept his salvation by faith.

Christians face tremendous pressures — from the devil, the world, and even the church! It's all part of God's work to refine and prepare you for eternity. May you continue to stand firm!

Chapter 3 Love Hurts
2 Corinthians 2:1-4

¹So I made up my mind that I would not make another painful visit to you. ²For if I grieve you, who is left to make me glad but you whom I have grieved? ³ I wrote as I did, so that when I came I would not be distressed by those who should have made me rejoice. I had confidence in all of you, that you would all share my joy. ⁴ For I wrote you out of great distress and anguish of heart and with many tears, not to grieve you but to let you know the depth of my love for you.

A broken heart. You probably already know that loving someone can be painful. Just because you love them does not mean you overlook problems in the relationship. If you read through the two Corinthian letters you know there were lots of problems in Paul's relationship with the Corinthian church, but he doesn't just let the competing apostles take over. He had plenty of justification to walk away and busy himself with countless other ministry opportunities. He could have avoided so much pain.

But real love, *agape* love (the Greek word used here for God-like, unconditional love), doesn't give up. Just because you have serious problems in your marriage doesn't mean you give your wife up to that other man and walk away. God doesn't expect you to put up with that abusive husband, but divorce is not his solution. God wants to change that man! Avoiding pain doesn't really deal with the pain. Just because you have issues with the church you're pastoring doesn't mean you resign and move on. God has a purpose in the pain. We grow as we confront the issues and work through them.

And yet there are times when we need to stay away for a while. Being together can be so painful that healing isn't possible at the moment. I hate to say it, but that can mean separation from your spouse – but only with the goal of healing and restoring the relationship. It may mean a sabbatical from your church. It is the ones we love most who hurt us the most, but they are also the ones who bring us the most joy. Hence Paul writes that the Corinthians should be the ones who make him rejoice. If he damages the relationship too much, he will lose the very ones who could make him glad. Unfortunately, men seem prone to do that when dealing with their wives and children.

In this letter Paul backs off the strong words which made a previous letter - and his last visit – so painful. He had hoped that letter would settle things so when he saw them everything would be fine. It didn't turn out that way. Now he has to trust that somehow God was in it, and will bring restoration. In the meantime, these few verses are full of pain. Look at the words he uses: *"grieve"* (3 times); *"distress"* (twice); *"painful;" "anguish;" "many tears."* Love hurts.

Are you in a painful relationship right now? Are you tempted to walk away? Do you feel hopeless? Does the pain seem more than you can bear? We are experts at avoiding pain through alcohol, drugs and medication, or busyness.

Chapter 3 Love Hurts

God wants to meet you in your pain and give you the strength to endure and keep loving. You're right – you can't do it on your own. But here you have a chance to learn God-like, agape, love. That's the kind of love Paul had for this difficult church; the same kind of love men are commanded to have for their wives as we lay down our lives for them. Be encouraged, my brother! God is moving us beyond our self-centeredness, calling us to the cross, and then giving us new life and a love like we have never known before. My sister, Jesus wants to pour out his love on you in the midst of your pain. You have the power within you to love and impact your family, your church, and your world. Love never fails and never gives up. God wants to give you faith and hope – but most importantly, love.

Chapter 4 Insights into Church Discipline
2 Corinthians 2:5-11

⁵ I am not overstating it when I say that the man who caused all the trouble hurt all of you more than he hurt me. ⁶ Most of you opposed him, and that was punishment enough. ⁷ Now, however, it is time to forgive and comfort him. Otherwise he may be overcome by discouragement. ⁸ So I urge you now to reaffirm your love for him.

⁹ I wrote to you as I did to test you and see if you would fully comply with my instructions. ¹⁰ When you forgive this man, I forgive him, too. And when I forgive whatever needs to be forgiven, I do so with Christ's authority for your benefit, ¹¹ so that Satan will not outsmart us. For we are familiar with his evil schemes. (NLT)

"This man" may be the brother in Paul's first letter who was disciplined for an incestuous relationship. The Corinthian church followed his instructions, and now Paul is concerned that they might take it too far. It's time to move toward restoration.

Six important lessons about church discipline

1. We need to know when to end the discipline. Unfortunately, some believers are like abusive parents who

take delight in seeing the person suffer. There is little love, and the focus is more on punishment than restoration. Discipline always needs to be exercised under the supervision of elders, a pastor, or an apostle; someone directly involved with the person who knows when the discipline should end.

2. The danger is that the person disciplined might be overwhelmed by excessive sorrow, fall into despair, and give up on the church. The goal instead is godly sorrow which brings repentance and leads to salvation, which Paul speaks of later in the letter (7:10). Chrysostom, the early church father, wrote: "Some [believers] Satan destroys through sin, others through the unmeasured sorrow following on repentance for it…conquering with our own weapons." If you've come back to the Lord after falling into sin, be careful of overwhelming, excessive, sorrow. Once you repent and the Lord forgives you, sorrow should be replaced by joy. Any other reaction may be the devil's condemnation. Unfortunately, the church can play right into the devil's schemes by continuing to shun the repentant sinner.

3. Discipline ends, and the church must purposefully forgive and comfort the restored sinner - publicly embracing and encouraging him. Love is reaffirmed, the transgression is forgotten, and he is joyfully welcomed back into full fellowship. That may not be easy if the person caused problems for the church, and may test the church's willingness to obey Christ's command to forgive. Failure to forgive can make the hypocritical church member a worse sinner than the one who was disciplined!

4. Beyond the need to deal with the sin, Paul had another purpose in commanding the discipline: testing their heart attitude. Some believers might question if this test was appropriate, insisting that they need to obey God alone. God tests us to see how fully we will obey him. Often that obedience is to someone he has placed in authority over us.

5. Since the Corinthians did obey him, Paul assures them he will honor their decision to cease the discipline and forgive the offender. The apostle or supervisor needs to have similar respect for the church which is under their care.

6. Unforgiveness opens the door to Satan, who loves to keep people under condemnation. He robs them of peace and forgiveness, creates division, and sows rebellion in the hearts of those who feel the discipline is too severe. Paul is well aware that Satan is crafty and can easily outwit us. We must keep our guard up and be aware of all his schemes.

Is the Spirit speaking to you? To forgive someone? To affirm your love for them? To comfort them? Have you fallen into despair – unknowingly dragged into Satan's web of condemnation? Are there ways he's trying to outwit you right now? Are you aware of his schemes?

Chapter 5 Insights into the Ministry
2 Corinthians 2:12-17

¹² Now when I went to Troas to preach the gospel of Christ and found that the Lord had opened a door for me, ¹³ I still had no peace of mind, because I did not find my brother Titus there. So I said goodbye to them and went on to Macedonia.

Let's follow Paul's steps as he seeks to serve the Lord:

- He goes to a new city on an apostolic journey.
- He goes with the best of purposes: to preach the gospel of Christ.
- God himself opened a door for him in that city.
- Yet he was unable to stay and minister there.
- The emptiness he felt without Titus was too great.
- He had no peace of mind – and apparently peace of mind is important as we minister.
- So he moves on to Macedonia.

The importance of relationships in ministry

Are you surprised that Paul would be guided by something as subjective as "peace of mind"? We might expect him to miss Titus and struggle to continue with the ministry, but many of us would feel obligated to push on through the door which God opened. We'd put aside our feelings and preach, despite the emptiness we felt. Not Paul. Relationships are extremely important! Are you lonely in ministry? Do you have a Titus to work with you? Have you felt obligated to push on, even though you lack peace of mind? Is it time to move to a place where you can work together with your Titus and have that peace of mind?

14 But thanks be to God, who always leads us as captives in Christ's triumphal procession and uses us to spread the aroma of the knowledge of him everywhere. 15 For we are to God the pleasing aroma of Christ among those who are being saved and those who are perishing. 16 To the one we are an aroma that brings death; to the other, an aroma that brings life. And who is equal to such a task?

Christ's triumphal procession

So far this letter has seemed anything but triumphant. Paul is hurting because of problems with the Corinthians. He has gone through such tremendous hardship that he felt he was going to die. There have been unexpected changes in his plans, causing others to question whether God is really leading him. Yet he is confident he is in a triumphal procession led by Christ.

Paul is probably referring to the victory parades a returning general or emperor would lead, bringing captives with them. During the parade, incense may have been offered to their god in thanksgiving. It was a pleasing aroma to the victors, but the fragrance of defeat and death to the captives. As God's captive, we may not always go where we want to go.

Whether you like it or not, you bring Christ's aroma with you wherever you go. Its intensity is probably determined by how full of the Spirit you are. That may be why people under the enemy's dominion avoid you, and why at times they actually smell foul. On the other hand, you may notice a faint sweet aroma in church or around Spirit-filled believers.

What a privilege to be part of Christ's triumphal procession! Are you his captive? Do you spread the knowledge of Christ everywhere you go? Can you confidently say he's leading you? Even Paul knew that the task was daunting – but God equips us for it. There is nothing we can do to smell good – it is Christ in us that brings this pleasing aroma. How do you smell? Do you bring life to those you meet?

Saved – or being saved?

There is an interesting use of the progressive tense in those "being saved" and those who are "perishing." We like to think of salvation as something that is accomplished the moment we accept Christ – and in a sense it is. But it is also a process, as we continue to follow Christ in his triumphant procession. If we get out of line we can start to smell like death. Others may look alive, but are in the process of perishing – unless they are snatched from the flames.

Why are you in ministry?

[17] *Unlike so many, we do not peddle the word of God for profit. On the contrary, in Christ we speak before God with sincerity, as those sent from God.*

Hucksters. Charlatans. Unfortunately, not everyone who preaches the word smells so great. There are many doing their own thing, from less than sincere motives. They have not been sent from God. One sure way to smell a rat is the focus on money. They are ministering for their own profit. That may involve financial gain or personal fame. To speak in Christ's name and preach his Word is an awesome responsibility.

Would you say you minister in full sincerity? How about the leaders in your church? If we are honest there will usually be a mixture of motives in our ministry. Examine your motives – and make the necessary adjustments if most of them are selfish. When you preach, do you do it to impress the people, or to please God? Can you confidently say God has sent you where you are, and that what you are doing is "in Christ"?

Chapter 6 Ever-increasing Glory
2 Corinthians 3

Life and ministry are a struggle – even for the Christian, and even for a great apostle like Paul. So far in this letter Paul has focused on his struggles: Conflicts with the Corinthians, suffering that made him despair of life, and constant opposition. But now we get a glimpse of what God is doing that makes it bearable.

The real recommendation for ministry

First, we must see beyond what the world values as "recommendations" and focus on what is important to God.

¹Are we beginning to commend ourselves again? Or do we need, like some people, letters of recommendation to you or from you? ² You yourselves are our letter, written on our hearts, known and read by everyone. ³ You show that you are a letter from Christ, the result of our ministry, written not with ink but with the Spirit of the living God, not on tablets of stone but on tablets of human hearts.

It is common for a new church member or someone wanting to do ministry to bring a letter of recommendation from another church or a well-known leader. They may have a certificate of ordination or an academic degree. That's good. But it's not enough. Apparently Paul's opponents in Corinth had that. Unfortunately, things are not always as they seem. Someone with glowing recommendations and credentials may have been a child molester. Ordination papers can be bought on the internet. And a seminary degree says little about the person's character.

For something as precious as ministry to Christ's body, rigorous standards need to be followed. To become a minister in my denomination you have to be recommended by your local church. Then the council of pastors and elders in that area takes you under its care - if they agree that God is calling you to the ministry. The council mentors you, examines you, and helps you prepare for your calling. That usually includes formal studies, but seminary professors also need to issue a "Certificate of Fitness for Ministry", based on the person's walk with the Lord and demonstration of Christian character. All that is good – especially today, when someone can start a church with virtually no preparation or accountability. But it still is not enough.

Jesus said to examine their fruit (Matthew 7:16-20; 12:33; John 15:1-16). He seems to refer primarily to you lasting impact on others' lives, including their salvation and spiritual health. The fruit of the Spirit (Galatians 5:22-23) are also important. Other New Testament references to fruit in our lives are Ephesians 5:9, Philippians 1:11, Colossians 1:6 & 10, and James 3:17. Paul is concerned with what is in people's hearts, not with letters. Your real letter of recommendation is the people you have ministered to, and the Spirit's transforming work in their lives. TV and internet ministry can look impressive, but you never see the real fruit - the letters written on human hearts. If you are considering someone for a position in your church or ministry, get to know the church they served and the people they ministered to. That is their most important recommendation.

⁴ Such confidence we have through Christ before God. ⁵ Not that we are competent in ourselves to claim anything for ourselves, but our competence comes from God. ⁶ He has made us competent as ministers of a new covenant—not of the letter but of the Spirit; for the letter kills, but the Spirit gives life.

God makes you competent!

Competence. The very word causes anxiety for many people. How about you? That common feeling of incompetence leads people do all kinds of things to prove to themselves or others that they have what it takes. They point to test results and job evaluations. There certainly is a place for developing abilities in your profession. But we are not like people in the world who have to project competence to keep their jobs. When it comes to ministry, Paul says you *don't* have to prove your competence. In fact, feel free to confess you're *not* competent in yourself! You *don't* have what it takes! Whatever competence you have comes from God – and when God calls you to a position, he *makes you competent*! As long as you rely on him, he supplies everything you need. What freedom! No wonder Paul says the letter kills! Maybe you have labored under the pressure of performing a certain way and felt that death. The pressure's off! Relax, love God and other people, and allow his strength and anointing to flow through you.

⁷ The old way, with laws etched in stone, led to death, though it began with such glory that the people of Israel could not bear to look at Moses' face. For his face shone with the glory of God, even though the brightness was already fading away. [8] Shouldn't we expect far greater glory under the new way, now that the Holy Spirit is giving life? [9] If the old way, which brings condemnation, was glorious, how much more glorious is the new way, which makes us right with God! [10] In fact, that first glory was not glorious at all compared with the overwhelming glory of the new way. [11] So if the old way, which has been replaced, was glorious, how much more glorious is the new, which remains forever! (NLT)

Christian ministry is glorious!

Remember how Israel couldn't approach Mount Sinai because of God's glorious presence? A pillar of fire led the people in the wilderness, Moses' face reflected God's glory, and the glory cloud filled the tabernacle (Exodus 13:21-22; 34:29-36; 40:34; 2 Chronicles 5:14; 7:2). That was the Old Covenant of law on stone tablets - a ministry that brought death and condemnation. It doesn't begin to compare to the glory of the New Covenant of righteousness and life, adoption into God's family, and the fullness of the Spirit! And this glory lasts –unlike Moses' fading glory.

Is that how you see your ministry? Has church become so routine that you no longer see the glory? Open your eyes and see your ministry as glorious as God says it is!

[12] Therefore, since we have such a hope, we are very bold. [13] We are not like Moses, who would put a veil over his face to prevent the Israelites from seeing the end of what was passing away. [14] But their minds were made dull, for to this day the same veil remains when the old covenant is read. It

Chapter 6 Ever-increasing Glory

has not been removed, because only in Christ is it taken away. ¹⁵ Even to this day when Moses is read, a veil covers their hearts. ¹⁶ But whenever anyone turns to the Lord, the veil is taken away. ¹⁷ Now the Lord is the Spirit, and where the Spirit of the Lord is, there is freedom.

Understanding the glorious nature of New Covenant ministry, we boldly come before the Lord and bring him to others. We are helping people see God! We are presenting Christ, who removes the veil from their hearts! We are offering them freedom, and the Lord's presence!

If this ministry is so glorious, why is it so hard for people to receive it? Satan has veiled the minds of unbelievers. It is when we pray, wage warfare, preach the Word, or minister in the power of the Spirit that people turn to the Lord. When they do, the veil is removed.

¹⁸ And we all, who with unveiled faces contemplate the Lord's glory, are being transformed into his image with ever-increasing glory, which comes from the Lord, who is the Spirit.

Have you ever questioned whether the Holy Spirit is fully God? The Lord *is* the Spirit. Paul says it twice for emphasis! When the Spirit indwells you, God himself is living in you. And he is hard at work transforming you into his image. That process can be painful at times, but if you contemplate God's glory, looking to him, worshipping him, and living in his presence, the pain will be swallowed up in glory. How is that process going in your life? Can others see God's image in you? Can you see God's image in the people you are ministering to? There should be ever-increasing glory. All too often there can be setbacks in that process and the veil comes back, blinding us to what God is doing. Rip the veil off! Seek the glory of God! Look at him – and get back on track, allowing that glory to keep increasing!

Chapter 7 We do not Lose Heart
2 Corinthians 4

Do you ever struggle with discouragement? Most people probably fight it much of their lives. Paul did. But despite the many reasons he had to be discouraged, in the first verse, and again in verse 16, Paul says "We do not lose heart." The Greek word can mean "discouraged, spiritless and despondent with fear, or faint with weariness and exhaustion." What had Paul learned that enabled him to not lose heart?

[1]Therefore, since through God's mercy we have this ministry, we do not lose heart. [2]Rather, we have renounced secret and shameful ways; we do not use deception, nor do we distort the word of God. On the contrary, by setting forth the truth plainly we commend ourselves to everyone's conscience in the sight of God. [3]And even if our gospel is veiled, it is veiled to those who are perishing. [4]The god of this age has blinded the minds of unbelievers, so that they cannot see the light of the gospel that displays the glory of Christ, who is the image of God. [5]For what we preach is not ourselves, but Jesus Christ as Lord, and ourselves as your servants for Jesus' sake. [6]For God, who said, "Let light shine out of darkness," made his light shine in our hearts to give us the light of the knowledge of God's glory displayed in the face of Christ.

Understand the privilege and responsibility of sharing in the glorious Gospel ministry

Paul starts the chapter with "therefore." To understand this passage, then, we have to see what the "therefore" is there for. Chapter divisions in the Bible were inserted later and can interrupt the flow of thought. God's glory fills the end of chapter three, as Paul speaks about the glory of Christian ministry and God transforming us into his image. If we can see beyond the struggles of ministry to get that vision, and realize that even in the hard times God is molding us into the image of Christ, it will help us not to lose heart. Paul is well aware he has done nothing to deserve participation in that divine work. The privilege of sharing in God's glory has been given to Paul by a merciful God, so Paul is responsible to serve him to the best of his ability.

Expose the god of this age and renounce his work

Given the exalted nature of the ministry, Paul is obligated to confront anyone using secret and shameful ways, deceiving the people, and distorting the Word of God. He endures persistent opposition and persecution, and is under such pressure that death is his constant companion. Why is life so hard if he is doing God's will? He is fighting Satan, the god of this age. The devil's servants will do whatever is necessary to advance their agenda. The focus is off Jesus. They exalt themselves and preach a man-centered gospel. The devil, a master deceiver and the father of lies, happily veils the minds of unbelievers and even Christians.

We know that our God is the only Lord of this universe and Satan is no god at all. But the devil has been given authority

Chapter 7 We do not Lose Heart

on earth. We are operating in enemy territory. Americans have tried to hold onto the idea that the United States is a Christian country, but it's becoming harder to avoid the reality that Satan is the god of this age, and we are proclaiming a kingdom that is not of this world. The world increasingly laughs at the truths that seem so obvious to us, because Satan is doing such a great job blinding them. We have made his job easy by preaching a man-centered gospel and failing to clearly present Jesus in word, deed, and power. We are often so caught up looking at what the world offers that we don't see Jesus' face full of God's glory, nor do we reflect that glory to the world. Instead we look like religious legalists who will not let them enjoy life.

It is easy to get discouraged when you relentlessly face this kind of false Christianity. It can be tempting to join the party and get the acclaim and money others are getting. Paul's response is to renounce those tactics, focus on the truth of the Gospel, and present the Word as clearly as possible. Understanding the nature of the battle can keep us from losing heart.

⁷ But we have this treasure in jars of clay to show that this all-surpassing power is from God and not from us. ⁸ We are hard pressed on every side, but not crushed; perplexed, but not in despair; ⁹ persecuted, but not abandoned; struck down, but not destroyed. ¹⁰ We always carry around in our body the death of Jesus, so that the life of Jesus may also be revealed in our body. ¹¹ For we who are alive are always being given over to death for Jesus' sake, so that his life may also be revealed in our mortal body. ¹² So then, death is at work in us, but life is at work in you.

Accept that suffering and weakness are part of this life – and keep going anyway

As if there wasn't enough pressure from outside to deal with, there is also a constant inner struggle. God has chosen to use our fragile bodies to carry the treasure of the Gospel. Through aging and sickness – the very things our culture does everything in its power to resist – we find ourselves physically broken and wasting away. And these clay jars can also be emotionally fragile. Struggles with depression and even suicide are common among Christians. Discouragement is a constant struggle for most Christians. Although each battle may be different, we all face many things that could make us lose heart. Paul was:

- Hard pressed on every side – feeling seemingly relentless pressure on every front
- Perplexed – unable to make sense of what's going on; confused
- Persecuted
- Struck down

What a way for a great apostle and man of faith like Paul to live, constantly on the edge! Health and wealth preachers must have a hard time with this chapter! God almost sadistically allowed these struggles - but in each case he also gave the strength to endure, and in the process draw closer to him. How did God help him endure?

- The pressure stopped just short of Paul being crushed

Chapter 7 We do not Lose Heart

- Paul didn't get to the point of total despair and give up
- Paul was always aware of God's presence with him in the persecution
- Paul's body could be bloodied and broken – but not completely destroyed

What's more, Paul constantly lived with death. The cross of Christ did not just hang on a chain around his neck. The cross was not remembered just once a year on Good Friday. Paul *always* carried around Christ's death in his body. It may have been pain, his thorn in the flesh, or some life-long infirmity. He was *always* being given over to death.

Much as we talk about our hope of heaven, many of us are afraid of death. We have a hard time with hospitals and funerals. But the Christian lives with death as his constant companion. We are to die to self daily, crucifying the flesh and its sinful habits. What a contrast to the way our culture pampers the body: muscles sculpted through hours at the gym, stomachs full of gourmet food, and skin massaged and moisturized with expensive lotions.

How do Paul's struggles compare with the challenges you are facing? Do you find it encouraging to realize you may not have it all that bad?

It's not about you – it's all about Jesus

As we die and get out of the picture, Jesus is able to reveal himself more and more in our mortal bodies. He makes us less self-centered and can demonstrate his power, so there is no doubt who is at work. No wonder the world doesn't see

Jesus in us! We are too busy keeping our distance from death! Just as Jesus willingly gave up his life for us, Paul is willing to face death so others can experience life. Do we selfishly fight death and thus deprive others of experiencing Christ's life? We in America have come a long way from the conviction that the blood of martyrs is the seed of the church. Meanwhile Jesus is being revealed and glorified as never before in many nations where persecution, suffering, and death are part of daily life.

Suffering should not silence us. In fact, we are obligated to continue preaching the Gospel!

13 It is written: "I believed; therefore I have spoken." Since we have that same spirit of faith, we also believe and therefore speak, 14 because we know that the one who raised the Lord Jesus from the dead will also raise us with Jesus and present us with you to himself. 15 All this is for your benefit, so that the grace that is reaching more and more people may cause thanksgiving to overflow to the glory of God.

Think of heaven and God's glory

Knowing that Jesus rose from the grave, we have full assurance that death has been defeated and we are destined for heaven. We have to share that message of salvation with as many as possible, so God will be glorified through an outpouring of thanksgiving and praise. Do you share Paul's passion that multitudes would give thanks to God and glorify him?

16 Therefore we do not lose heart. Though outwardly we are wasting away, yet inwardly we are being renewed day by

Chapter 7 We do not Lose Heart

day. *¹⁷ For our light and momentary troubles are achieving for us an eternal glory that far outweighs them all. ¹⁸ So we fix our eyes not on what is seen, but on what is unseen, since what is seen is temporary, but what is unseen is eternal.*

Keep perspective – fix your eyes on the unseen

If you look at what's happening around you, you will get discouraged and lose heart. I can guarantee it! It is so easy to lose perspective. And so hard to fix our eyes on what is unseen, because what we can see is literally in our face. In America, what we see is usually very appealing, from that sporty new car to the comfortable house and giant screen TV. If you were living in a war-torn country it might be easier to focus on the unseen. I know it's hard to believe at times, but the troubles you are experiencing really are not that bad, and they are only temporary. God is still in control, and while death may be your constant companion, God is also constantly renewing you. Whatever dies in us allows his resurrection power to be displayed. The eternal glory awaiting you will make you forget all the pain.

Don't lose heart! Get your eyes off yourself and your circumstances, and focus on what is unseen!

Chapter 8 Are You Ready for Something Totally Different?

2 Corinthians 5:1-10

¹For we know that if the earthly tent we live in is destroyed, we have a building from God, an eternal house in heaven, not built by human hands. ² Meanwhile we groan, longing to be clothed instead with our heavenly dwelling, ³ because when we are clothed, we will not be found naked. ⁴ For while we are in this tent, we groan and are burdened, because we do not wish to be unclothed but to be clothed instead with our heavenly dwelling, so that what is mortal may be swallowed up by life. ⁵ Now the one who has fashioned us for this very purpose is God, who has given us the Spirit as a deposit, guaranteeing what is to come.

In chapter four Paul compared our bodies to jars of clay. Jars are great for storing water or food, but it's not too encouraging if you're looking for strength and endurance. Now he gives another metaphor that's not much better: tents.

What we know about this tent:

- It can be destroyed; it's mortal.
- It's built by human hands.
- It's uncomfortable – we're burdened, and groan in it.

- It's earthly.
- People generally don't live in tents. They are used temporarily on the way somewhere else.
- A storm, a wild animal, or a madman can rip up a tent and harm you. Tents are fragile and leave you vulnerable.
- Tents are subject to leaks and tears.

In stark contrast to this earthly tent, God has an eternal dwelling awaiting you in heaven. It is custom built for you, and nothing can harm it. It will cover you, protect you, and make you complete. When you put it on, your mortality is swallowed up in the pure life God designed you for. He didn't intend you to be subject to the pain, sickness, and mortality of this body. In fact, this body is so inadequate we feel naked in it. We try everything we can think of to patch up this tent and make it comfortable, but in the end it can't work. We have this nagging sense that there must be more! So we feel burdened and groan. Some people curse God because of the pain, but we really should thank him. He has the perfect provision prepared for us. If we were too comfortable in this tent, we wouldn't long for our eternal dwelling and beautiful new clothes. Those clothes will be better than the most expensive fashions available today. In fact, our clothes are so inadequate that we're essentially parading around naked. I wonder if God doesn't laugh at our attempts to glamorously cover ourselves!

How can you be certain that this heavenly dwelling is actually waiting for you? Paul refers back to the same guarantee he presented in 1:22: the Holy Spirit. When something is repeated in Scripture it's for a reason. He wants to strengthen your hope and give you great security! If your experience in the Spirit is deficient, you may find it hard to accept this guarantee. But when you truly taste the Spirit, he gives you great confidence that the guarantee is real.

As we age and our tents become worn and our clay jars crack, this promise becomes all the more important. You may be young and feel you have a great tent that will see you through any storm, but God often allows bad storms to show our tents' vulnerability. In illness and brokenness we groan and long to be clothed in our eternal dwelling. This is a normal part of life, as we get ready to make the transition to eternity.

[6] Therefore we are always confident and know that as long as we are at home in the body we are away from the Lord. [7] For we live by faith, not by sight. [8] We are confident, I say, and would prefer to be away from the body and at home with the Lord.

This is a real dilemma. All we've ever known is this tent, and, for the most part, it has served us well. Frankly, although I would change a few things, I like my tent. Despite the glory of our heavenly home, our tendency is to try and hold on to the tent. But our experience of the Spirit gives us confidence, and eventually pushes us to the point of preferring to be with the Lord. In the meantime there are three important things that will help you make the most of this life and best prepare you for eternity:

1. **Don't trust your eyes.** Trust the Lord and his Word. Be wary of what makes sense to you and is endorsed by this world. Fill your mind with thoughts of God and his kingdom.

2. **Get your priorities straight.** What is your number one goal in life? It's fine to make goals, but your first priority should be to please the Lord. That is truly important - and will impact your eternity. To do this you have to know what pleases him, which we learn by studying the Bible - and hopefully hearing it taught in church. When you love someone you want to please that person. It's not burdensome. When you please your spouse you get pleasure from their delight, and reap benefits in return. God gets true pleasure when he sees his sons and daughters seeking to please him, even if they are not always successful!

3. **We have much to look forward to in heaven, and it is guaranteed.** God is a loving Father who delights in preparing good things for us. But remember he is also a just judge, whom we need to revere with a holy fear. Your salvation is secure as long as you continue to trust in Christ and honor him as Lord. Even then you will still stand before his judgment seat to receive what is due you – both good and bad. There will be rewards and levels of authority given, depending on what you did in this life. That is sobering - and should make us think twice about doing something we know displeases him. Your primary motive should be love for God, but, just as your boss pays you for your earthly work, God is a totally fair heavenly boss and will give you exactly what he owes you.

Chapter 8 Are You Ready for Something Totally Different?

Are you excited? Is this a new perspective for you? Our tents have become so elaborate and our lives here so comfortable that this may all seem very distant and unreal. It tends to grow in importance as we age, but you never know when you will depart this tent to be with the Lord. Don't delay putting these guidelines into practice!

Chapter 9 The Ministry of Reconciliation
2 Corinthians 5:9-21

How do you feel about evangelism? Guilty? Scared? Excited? Passionate? Or is it better left to fanatics? Evangelism is simply telling others about Jesus. The inevitable result of receiving the Spirit's power is being a witness to Jesus everywhere you go (Acts 1:8). It doesn't require knocking on doors, accosting strangers, or street corner preaching. There is no prescribed formula of what to say. Jesus said he would make us fishers of men – not hunters (Matthew 4:19). We put out bait, and if there's a nibble we proceed. Study Jesus and the way he interacted with people.

In this passage Paul gives nine convincing reasons to be passionate about evangelism.

⁹ So we make it our goal to please him, whether we are at home in the body or away from it.

1. **Your goal in life is to please God.** Jesus said if you are ashamed of him before men he will be ashamed of you before his Father (Matthew 10:32, Mark 8:38, Luke 9:26). It pleases God when you have the faith and willingness to tell others about the great things Jesus has done for you. The angels in heaven rejoice when someone comes to Christ

(Luke 15:10). God is not pleased when he gives you an opportunity to speak up for him and you fail to do so.

¹⁰ For we must all appear before the judgment seat of Christ, so that each of us may receive what is due us for the things done while in the body, whether good or bad.

2. **You tell others about Jesus not only because you're excited about him and love him, but also because you have a healthy fear of God.** You will have to give an account for opportunities to share the Gospel you passed up:

> *When I say to the wicked, 'You wicked person, you will surely die,' and you do not speak out to dissuade them from their ways, that wicked person will die for their sin, and I will hold you accountable for their blood. But if you do warn the wicked person to turn from their ways and they do not do so, they will die for their sin, though you yourself will be saved* (Ezekiel 33:8 & 9).

On the positive side, you will be rewarded for all you do in Jesus' name, from giving a cup of cold water to sharing the Gospel. (Matthew 10:40-42)

¹¹ Since, then, we know what it is to fear the Lord, we try to persuade others. What we are is plain to God, and I hope it is also plain to your conscience. ¹² We are not trying to commend ourselves to you again, but are giving you an opportunity to take pride in us, so that you can answer those who take pride in what is seen rather than in what is in the heart. ¹³ If we are "out of our mind," as some say, it is for God; if we are in our right mind, it is for you.

3. **Paul's fear of God helped him to endure great suffering and tirelessly preach Jesus.** He calls it "trying to persuade others." There is a great case for believing the Gospel, and Paul wasn't afraid to debate and engage the brightest minds of his day. Are you familiar enough with the Bible and why you believe to feel confident trying to persuade someone? Or are you afraid they might come up with something that demolishes your faith, or ask a question you can't answer? You have a responsibility to study and prepare to effectively evangelize, so you don't make a fool out of yourself or Jesus. If you don't know the answer, be honest and tell them you will find out. And then make sure you do.

Paul never tried to hide who he was. Too many Christians go about their day incognito! You don't have to wear a huge cross or Jesus T-shirts. What you are should be plain from your lifestyle and speech. God is not fooled by attempts to put on a religious show in church while you are somebody else with your friends. Be transparent – so the world can see Jesus in you. If it doesn't see him, ask yourself what part Jesus really has in your life.

Fanatic. Jesus freak. Crazy. People were quick to say Paul was out of his mind - especially his family and friends in the Jewish establishment, where he could have lived very comfortably as a rabbi. Anyone who is really serious about Jesus will probably look crazy to the world. Even Jesus' mother said he was out of his mind (Mark 3:21)! Don't let the world's labels deter you from being open about your beliefs. It can be especially hard today, with the pressure to accept different lifestyles and religions. One survey found 65% of American Christians believe other religions can lead to God (pewforum.org)! Increasingly, you will be looked at as a fanatic if you stand for what the Bible says.

Most people take pride in what they see: clothes, cars, and gadgets. You can have all the world's toys and still have an ugly, empty, heart. Be sure you don't get caught up in this visible world. When people get tired of all the externals and realize their hearts are broken or empty, be ready to tell them about somebody who can mend and fill that heart. What is in your heart that will show the world you are different, and draw people to Jesus?

[14] For Christ's love compels us, because we are convinced that one died for all, and therefore all died.

4. **Love. Christ's love, which you experience on a daily basis.** It is a love for others like you never had before – including love for even the ugliest sinner. It is knowing that God so loved the world that he gave his only Son, that whoever believes in him should be saved (John 3:16). But how can they believe if they haven't heard?

You know what will save someone from eternity in hell. How can you be so selfish that you won't tell them about it? If you had medicine that would heal people, would you keep it from them as they lay dying, especially if there were no cost to you? If you have any kind of human decency, let alone love, you are compelled to do whatever you can to let them know. Especially your friends and family. Can you really act like everything is fine, knowing the Bible says they will suffer eternally without Christ?

Chapter 9 The Ministry of Reconciliation

¹⁵ And he died for all, that those who live should no longer live for themselves but for him who died for them and was raised again.

5. Who are you living for? The world has taught you since childhood that you should live for yourself. Now you must go against that and live for Christ. Jesus didn't die just for you, or for an elect few. He died for all! If you are living for Jesus, self and all its concern about image and rejection are out of the picture. Time and energy are freed up to serve Jesus and care for others.

¹⁶ So from now on we regard no one from a worldly point of view. Though we once regarded Christ in this way, we do so no longer.

6. Your image of yourself and what is important has changed. Now you have a new way of seeing people. It's not about what they can do for you, how they look, or how well they measure up to the world's standards. You look at them as Jesus does, with a heart of compassion, acceptance, and unconditional love.

¹⁷ Therefore, if anyone is in Christ, he is a new creation: Old things have passed away and all things are made new!

7. You have the power to introduce people to a totally new life! All the sin and mistakes of the past can be wiped out as they are born again. What an incredible offer! This is truly good news! Are you living in that reality? Have you let go of all the "old things?" This can be especially powerful for older people with many regrets, who feel it is too late to start over or change their lives.

[18] All this is from God, who reconciled us to himself through Christ and gave us the ministry of reconciliation: [19] that God was reconciling the world to himself in Christ, not counting people's sins against them. And he has committed to us the message of reconciliation.

8. **Remember how you were alienated from God because of sin?** Under the Old Covenant the Jews had to make all kinds of sacrifices - and there was still no complete reconciliation. In Christ your relationship with the God of the universe is restored. Maybe you have heard it so often that you have forgotten how radical and amazing it is. God took the initiative and paid the extreme price of his own Son's life. He has wiped the slate clean, so you don't have to pay anything for all your sins. He did the work, but he does have some expectations of you. One is to let other people know about this amazing offer. It should be an easy sell, right? Think of all the junk people pay big money for! This is free! And he trusts you with this precious message! In fact, he has committed it to you! How do you think he would feel if you keep it to yourself and didn't let anyone know?

[20] We are therefore Christ's ambassadors, as though God were making his appeal through us. We implore you on Christ's behalf: Be reconciled to God.

9. **You have been appointed an ambassador of the Kingdom of Heaven.** If you still are not convinced, this is the clincher. Can you imagine the president calling you up and saying you have been selected as the U.S. ambassador to some foreign country? What would happen if you kept

Chapter 9 The Ministry of Reconciliation

going about your business and ignored him? This is far more important!

If I were to serve as a U.S. ambassador, I would represent the United States and have its authority. I would have to consult Washington to find out its policy and then relate that to the foreign government. I can't just say what makes sense to me. Even if I don't like what Washington says, I am still obligated to support it. You cannot be a self-appointed ambassador. If I were to go to the Mexican government, announcing that I was the new U.S. ambassador, they would ask for my credentials. If I couldn't produce any, I would be kicked out and probably investigated for impersonating a U.S. official.

Here's another example: If I were an authorized Ford dealer and I have sold out my inventory, I can call Ford and they will happily send me another shipment of cars. But I'm not a dealer. If I call them requesting more cars, they will laugh and hang up on me.

You, however, are authorized. You are commissioned. You don't need any special ordination service. You *are* Christ's ambassador. You have the full authority of God Almighty – just as the apostles did - to preach the Kingdom, heal the sick, and cast out demons. Are you faithfully representing your King?

21 God made him who had no sin to be sin for us, so that in him we might become the righteousness of God.

This is the Gospel in one verse: The perfect Son of God was made sin by his Father, bearing the sin of the world on our behalf, so we could be free from sin and become God's righteousness.

One of the greatest thrills is seeing someone repent and be born again! God wants to use you! There are people around you who desperately need him! Ask God to give you an opportunity to talk about him this week – and then put aside your fears and trust him to use you as his ambassador.

Chapter 10 Receiving God's Grace in Vain

2 Corinthians 6:1-2

¹As God's co-workers we urge you not to receive God's grace in vain. ² For he says,

*"In the time of my favor I heard you,
and in the day of salvation I helped you."*

I tell you, now is the time of God's favor, now is the day of salvation.

God is doing his part. You have his favor. He is listening. He has heard you. You are living in an age of grace, where his favor is poured out on us, even though we clearly don't deserve it. Judgment day is coming - but today is a day of salvation. He is available to help you. Think about all that for a minute. It is impressive!

Don't wait!

It is, however, a limited time offer. Don't delay. You don't know when his favor will be withdrawn. The day of salvation will end and judgment day will arrive. You may not always have God's ear. If you continually refuse his help, the time will come when it is no longer available. You have to receive what he is offering. You have been offered the most wonderful gift imaginable. It has been handed to you – but you have to receive it. It is great that Jesus paid for your sins on the cross. God himself longs to dwell in you and empower you through the Holy Spirit. But you must receive these gifts by faith. God's grace is available to you on a daily basis – but it does you no good when you insist on doing things in your own strength. You have to consciously choose to receive his grace.

What it means to receive God's grace in vain

What is perhaps most sobering is to receive his grace - but receive it in vain. God's grace is then unfruitful and has no impact on your life. A couple of years ago I gave my son a Groupon for rock climbing. He was excited about receiving it, but put off using it. It expired and the opportunity was lost. He received the gift in vain. I wasted my money, and he missed out on a good time. I was not very happy with him.

Let's think a little more about receiving God's gift in vain. Paul just explained all the benefits of new life in Christ, and our part in introducing others to him. Everything is made new. You are forgiven and reconciled to God, and you live for Christ. Considering that Paul was writing to Christians, it is strange that he *implores* them to be reconciled to God (5:20), and stresses the urgency of making that decision: *now* is the day of salvation (6:2). Paul apparently knew that despite the outpouring of God's grace in Corinth – both God's unmerited favor and the abundance of *charisms,* or spiritual gifts – there were many who had not experienced salvation. Our churches are full of decent people who have been part of church life for years - but have never been born again. They are still living for themselves and not for Christ. They are not serving as his ambassadors. There is still a lot of the unsaved person there. Maybe you are one of them. God may be opening your eyes right now to the need to come to the cross, give up, and fully hand control of your life over to him.

Empty faith with no effect

There is even more to this verse. The word translated vain can mean "empty, without effect, for nothing" (Oxford Dictionary). Paul uses it in 1 Corinthians 15:2: *By this gospel you are saved,* ***if*** *you hold firmly to the word I preach to you. Otherwise, you have believed* ***in vain.*** You can receive God's grace in vain, and you can believe in vain. Here the idea is hearing the good news and receiving it, but not firmly holding on to that word. Not persevering. In 1 Corinthians 15:10 Paul says he has received God's grace – and in his case it was *not* in vain. God's grace had its intended effect. How does he know that? His transformed life and hard work for Jesus provide evidence of its effectiveness. Then in verse 14 he says the Corinthians' faith is *useless* (same word) if Christ didn't rise from the dead.

Strange as it seems, it is possible to believe and receive God's grace, but that grace has no effect on your life. Have you known people like that? They make a decision and do all the usual Christian activities, but there is an emptiness. Their daily lives don't change. They are not holding onto the Word, obeying it, or walking by faith in it. Their lives deny the reality and purpose of God's grace. In that case the whole religious show is empty – they are doing it in vain.

Paul is concerned about that very thing with the Corinthians. The Christian walk requires effort on our part. If it didn't, Paul would not have spent so much time instructing, exhorting, and warning the Corinthian church.

So what do you have to do?

Some would say people who exhibit an empty faith were never really saved. In this passage (6:1-2), God clearly does his part, pouring out his grace and favor and doing everything possible to help us by filling us with his Holy Spirit. But we still have to do our part, by receiving, persevering, and living under Christ's lordship. Salvation begins with a decision, but it is much more than that. It is a life-long walk with Jesus.

God does not force people to accept him. He makes salvation available, and he may arrange circumstances that push us toward him. His Holy Spirit will open our eyes and draw us to him. But ultimately it is your decision. God relies on us to make this amazing offer known. We are his co-workers – an incredible privilege in itself. Just a few verses before Paul said we are on the same team; we are Christ's ambassadors. How are you doing as his co-worker? Is there someone you need to reach out to about getting his or her life in order? What are you doing with God's gifts? Are you using them for his glory and kingdom? Today is a day of salvation and God's favor. Receive that salvation and allow it to have its transforming impact on your life.

Chapter 11 The Ups and Downs of Serving Christ

2 Corinthians 6:3-11

Stumbling blocks

³ We put no stumbling block in anyone's path, so that our ministry will not be discredited.

Stumbling blocks hurt Christians, bring reproach to Christ's name among unbelievers, and discredit whole ministries. Our paths are rocky enough without believers, and especially Christian leaders, making them harder! Jesus promises severe judgment for any who cause his "little ones" to stumble (Matthew 18:6).

- Do you conduct your daily life and ministry determined not to be a stumbling block?
- Can you think of any stumbling block you have placed in someone's path? Can you remove it to make their walk easier?
- Have you suffered because someone was a knucklehead? Or because they used you for their own purposes and profit? Did you blame yourself for stumbling, when actually they tripped you up? Don't let them discourage you from following the Lord! It's not your fault!

If you have stumbled, God is reaching out to pick you up and help you move on. But don't be like a dog that returns to his vomit, going down the same path only to stumble again! Keep your eyes open, alert to ministries or leaders that are stumbling blocks.

How do you commend yourself?

[4] Rather, as servants of God we commend ourselves in every way.

Isn't it prideful to commend yourself? Apparently not! Not if you care about the people God has given you and see them in danger of being led astray. You may need to point out the errors and stand up for your ministry.

Who are they serving? God? Are they seeking to build his kingdom? Or are they on a self-serving power trip? Do they have Jesus' humble, foot-washing, servant's heart, or do they want to be served?

What are the ways Paul commends himself?

In great endurance; in troubles, hardships and distresses; [5] in beatings, imprisonments and riots; in hard work, sleepless nights and hunger;

That list doesn't seem too impressive. These are not what we usually associate with a great man of God, but they are reminders to the Corinthians of Paul's love and sacrifice in bringing them the Gospel.

How does your suffering for Christ compare?

Chapter 11 The Ups and Downs of Serving Christ

- Would you continue serving him if you knew you might end up in prison?
- How many beatings could you endure before looking for another job?
- Have you gone hungry and lost sleep because of your dedication to God's people?
- Do you have the endurance to keep going despite the constant hardship and distress the true servant of God encounters – not necessarily because of any sin or weakness?

Or have you embraced the widely-held lie that the Christian life is supposed to be easy and trouble-free? Be careful of success stories!

⁶In purity, understanding, patience and kindness; in the Holy Spirit and in sincere love; ⁷ in truthful speech and in the power of God; with weapons of righteousness in the right hand and in the left;

Do you stay patient, kind, and loving under stress? That's the fruit of the Holy Spirit. Do you stay pure and honest when internet porn beckons and lying seems the easy way out? A righteous life, combined with the power of the Spirit and weapons like the Word and prayer, is your best defense against the onslaughts of the world and the enemy. Though things around him were rough, Paul had an unshakable faith and fellowship with the Lord that gave him a powerful ministry.

The good and the bad

Paul's next statements are so extreme you might wonder if he were schizophrenic. Is your life ever like that, tossed back and forth on the waves? One day things seem glorious at your church and the next day you're ready to quit. You're madly in love one day and seemingly headed for divorce the next. We have been taught that life will be great if we do the right things. Negative experiences are evidence of sin, unbelief, or failure. If Paul's experience is any indication, ups and downs are part of life, and especially Christian leadership. Part of maturity is recognizing the truth in the old saying, "This too will pass." Don't despair on the down days, and thank God for the gift of good days.

*⁸through glory and dishonor,
bad report and good report;
genuine, yet regarded as impostors;
⁹ known, yet regarded as unknown;
dying, and yet we live on;
beaten, and yet not killed;
¹⁰ sorrowful, yet always rejoicing;
poor, yet making many rich;
having nothing, and yet possessing everything.*

We long for the good report, fame, happiness, and prosperity. But when Paul was martyred he had no material possessions or money. Many people looked down on him. Yet his legacy endures! Are you ready to embrace both extremes? Learn to base your feelings and worth in God instead of circumstances, popularity, or wealth. While things around you constantly change, Jesus remains the same. Rejoice in him even in the midst of crushing sorrow.

Chapter 11 The Ups and Downs of Serving Christ

Open hearts

¹¹ We have spoken freely to you, Corinthians, and opened wide our hearts to you. ¹² We are not withholding our affection from you, but you are withholding yours from us. ¹³ As a fair exchange—I speak as to my children—open wide your hearts also.

Paul sounds like God in many Old Testament prophecies (Isaiah 57:8, Ezekiel 16, Hosea 2) - an unrequited lover, rejected after doing so much for them. These are his spiritual children, and he longs for their love. You may be tempted to become bitter and close your heart to someone who has hurt you. The challenge in any relationship is to keep reaching out, as God does. That can be hard with so much opposition.

- Speak freely to the people you are ministering to. Be honest, giving them the whole counsel of God.
- Open your heart wide to love them.
- Don't withhold your affection, but love them as a parent loves their children.

I suspect Paul would say their rejection hurt more than all the beatings. If you have closed your heart and are withholding affection from a pastor or spiritual father who has disappointed you, trust God and open your heart wide. There may be someone, like Paul, who has given you a lot and is suffering from your rejection. God longs to restore those relationships.

Being a Christian – especially in ministry - presents constant challenges. There is nothing wrong with you because you are going through hard times. Be encouraged from Paul's example to stand firm, faithful to your calling.

Chapter 12 We are the Temple of the Living God
2 Corinthians 6:14-7:1

God's temple has to be clean and holy. But how far do we take holiness? What does it mean to be separate from the world? Some Christians have withdrawn to monasteries or Christian communes. Others will not go to movies, dances, or the beach – or even have TVs. There are women who don't wear pants. The Amish reject all modern conveniences and have little to do with outsiders. Those who break their rules are shunned.

Probably the vast majority of American Christians are closer to the other extreme. They feel free to drink – in moderation, of course. They don't think twice about going to an R-rated movie. They avoid the "worst" sins - but their lives look pretty much like every other American's, except they go to church and may read their Bible and listen to Christian music sometimes.

Jesus and holiness

Jesus was constantly in trouble for his association with "sinners." The Pharisees were aghast that he ate in a tax collector's house (Mark 2:14-16) or allowed a prostitute to pour oil on his feet (Luke 7:36-50). Yet Jesus never sinned, and always made clear that he expected his followers to stop sinning. In 1 Corinthians 5:9-10 Paul said we are to have nothing to do with are those who *call themselves Christians,* but continue to practice sin. He wasn't talking about people who never claimed to believe in Jesus, since we would have to withdraw from the world to avoid contact with "sinners," which Jesus never advocated.

Jesus was much more concerned with what's *inside* than the things that go on *outside* of us:

> *"Don't you see that whatever enters the mouth goes into the stomach and then out of the body? But the things that come out of a person's mouth come from the heart, and these defile them. For out of the heart come evil thoughts—murder, adultery, sexual immorality, theft, false testimony, slander. These are what defile a person; but eating with unwashed hands does not defile them."* (Matthew 15:17-20)

Jesus was merciless in his condemnation of the Pharisees' hypocrisy. He must grieve over the number of modern Pharisees in his church today, who, like their counterparts in the first century, miss what real holiness is all about. These few verses should open our understanding.

Unequally yoked

[14] *Do not be yoked together with unbelievers.*

This verse is most commonly applied to marriage, and rightfully so. The Old Covenant strictly prohibited God's people from marrying unbelievers. Intermarriage repeatedly got them in trouble; most notably Solomon, whose numerous foreign wives led him into idolatry. If Christ is the Lord and center of your life, how could you possibly choose to enter into a marriage covenant with someone who doesn't share your faith? If you are single, make a solemn commitment never to consider a relationship with an unbeliever, no matter how nice he or she may be. If you are already married to an unbeliever, Paul counsels us to stay in the marriage, unless the unbeliever chooses to leave.

The command, however, is not limited to marriage. It applies to any permanent, intimate, association; anything that involves a commitment and a close relationship which could lead to compromising your standards or threaten the purity of your devotion to Christ. That could be a business partnership, or anything that leaves you yoked together with an unbeliever. If you feel uneasy, it's probably the Holy Spirit warning you. Let the Spirit guide you in each situation.

Five examples of polar opposites

For what do righteousness and wickedness have in common?

One invites God's wrath and judgment, and took Christ to the cross. The other pleases him and should be the natural result of the new birth. Those who attempt to engage in both will experience intense inner conflict, quench the Holy Spirit, and find it impossible to come into God's presence.

The Greek word translated *"wickedness"* literally means *"lawlessness,"* referring to those who rebel against authority and are hell-bent (literally) on doing their own thing. Believers are committed to obeying God - submitting to him and the authorities he's instituted. There's no way lawlessness and submission can co-exist in an intimate relationship.

Or what fellowship can light have with darkness?

There is nothing wrong with having unbelieving friends, but don't expect to experience real fellowship with them. If you are truly living in the light and finding it hard to fellowship with certain believers, it may mean there is darkness in their lives. No matter how hard you try to promote unity and get together, you will find it just doesn't work. A spouse or child hiding sin in the darkness will disrupt your relationship. This often happens with men engaged in internet porn. On the other hand, there should be a natural fellowship with those who are walking in the light. How about you? Are you walking fully in the light, or are there things you need to confess, possibly to another brother or sister?

[15] *What harmony is there between Christ and Belial?*

Belial is a Hebrew word meaning "worthlessness," used in the Old Testament for Satan. Christ came to destroy the works of the devil. Christ and Satan are at war with each other, and you have probably been wounded in that warfare. If there is discord in your life, maybe you are trying to serve both Christ and the devil. That can also cause problems in a church or Christian organization. When Christ is lord there should be inner peace, and peace with other believers.

Or what does a believer have in common with an unbeliever?

Chapter 12 We are the Temple of the Living God

Today, probably a whole lot. They watch the same TV shows and movies, go to the same clubs, listen to the same music, and play the same video games. There should be a noticeable difference, although not necessarily in the external, legalistic way it has often been interpreted in the past.

[16]{} What agreement is there between the temple of God and idols?

Israel repeatedly got in trouble by worshipping idols. Very strict guidelines were given for the construction and maintenance of the Temple and the worship of God, just as clear guidelines are given for the church in the New Testament. There was no room for idols. And there's still no room for them. We usually don't have carved images in our homes or churches. Our idols today are money, entertainment, technology, and sex. We've tried to forge an agreement with them – when there is none.

You are God's temple

[16]For we are the temple of the living God.

You and me? Temples of the almighty God of the universe? You mean he doesn't need our fancy buildings? Could it be those buildings are really for us – and not for him at all? Do you grasp how radical this is? Your body is a temple of the Holy Spirit. Is it clean? Or polluted with sexual sin, excessive and unhealthy food, alcohol, or drugs and tobacco? A local body of believers – not their building – is also a temple of the Holy Spirit and needs to be treated with similar care.

Choose God

¹⁶As God has said:

*"I will live with them
and walk among them,
and I will be their God,
and they will be my people."*

You want to belong. You want a wife you can relate to for life. In the same way, from the beginning, God simply longs for a people who will acknowledge him for who he is and delight in him. He wants to live with us and walk among us! Is that your experience? The experience of your church? If not, is it possible you've gotten a little too cozy with the world, and God is no longer walking with you?

¹⁷ Therefore,

*"Come out from them
and be separate,
says the Lord.
Touch no unclean thing,
and I will receive you."*

To be received by God we have to repent, leave sin and the world behind, and be sanctified; separated unto him. We are not to even *touch* any unclean thing. What do you fill your mind with on the TV or internet? What kind of uncleanness is present in your life, your home, or your church? Is it time for some housecleaning? Could that be why God feels distant? He can't receive you until you make some bold decisions to separate yourself from the filth of the world!

Why the separation? So you can know God as your Father!

^{18} And,

*"I will be a Father to you,
and you will be my sons and daughters,
says the Lord Almighty."*

Do you want a dad? Have you always longed for a better relationship with your father? God is begging you to give him that place! He wants you to be his son or daughter! How can you turn your back on him? Maybe you have experienced a child's rejection. Imagine then how God is hurt by our rejection! He wants a family! But we keep insisting on breaking the family rules. We can't experience this beautiful, intimate, relationship while we are unequally yoked and enmeshed with the world.

Far from being a rigid "thou shalt not" religion, Christianity invites people into an intimate relationship with the Lord of the universe, and in doing so, a whole new family. Our family of origin is important, but when there is a conflict of allegiances, as there often will be, we stick with our new family. The privilege of being adopted into God's family, a co-heir with Christ, far outweighs whatever passing and ultimately unfulfilling pleasures we must forego in this world.

7:1Therefore, since we have these promises, dear friends, let us purify ourselves from everything that contaminates body and spirit, perfecting holiness out of reverence for God.

All these things are not just nice talk. They are promises God has made to you. They are an offer of the most incredible life imaginable. Aren't there enough unmarried Christians? Is it worth giving up all God offers you for eternity to be married to an unbeliever? Are the pornography and unclean things of this world really all that great?

Three things God is calling you to do:

- **Purify yourself from anything that contaminates your body.** How can it be that very spiritual people walk around grossly overweight from consuming food which we know destroys the body? Personally, I am vegan. For health reasons I have chosen a plant-based diet, avoiding all dairy and meat except for fish and seafood. I would never obligate others to make that choice, but I do encourage you to take a serious look at what you are putting into your body. It is a temple of the Holy Spirit and needs to be lovingly cared for as something holy, not something to abuse as we wish. The initial purification may include fasting to rid your body of toxins, various regimens to cleanse your digestive system, and certainly eliminating any illegal drugs or tobacco.
- **Purify yourself from everything that contaminates your spirit.** Conversations, books, magazines, TV shows, internet sites, video games, fantasies...the

list is long. The fact is we live in a spiritually polluted world, and it is very hard to avoid it! It would be great if we could simply wash and get rid of all the impurities in our minds, but our God-given memory functions very well. Things that contaminated my spirit 30 years ago can still come back vividly. Thank God for the blood of Jesus that cleanses us. Plead that blood over your life. Take a serious look at your mind, renounce every impurity you can think of, and ask for deliverance from its memory. Take inventory of what touches your spirit each day and determine to eliminate every contaminant. You may encounter resistance from your family and friends, but hang tough. It's worth it. Your spirit can also be contaminated by anger, bitterness, hatred, and unforgiveness. Ask God to reveal them and cleanse you.

- **Work toward complete holiness out of reverence for God.** None of us can claim to be completely holy, but we need to be on the way. If you have any fear of the Lord and the consequences of sin, any worship or reverence for him, or any love for him as your Father, make it your aim to be completely holy.

Where are you at today? Do you long for more intimacy with God – and other believers? Is it possible some of these things are standing in the way? Is it time to leave them behind and get out of an unequal yoke? Are you ready to get rid of the contaminants?

Chapter 13 The Value of Relationships
2 Corinthians 7:2-7

Intense.

Marked by or expressive of great zeal, energy, determination, or concentration. Exhibiting strong feeling or earnestness of purpose, deeply felt.

(Merriam-Webster Dictionary)

I would describe the Apostle Paul as intense. Intensity can lead to conflict and anxiety in relationships, as it did for Paul and the Corinthians. The great value he places on the relationship is evident:

² Make room for us in your hearts. We have wronged no one, we have corrupted no one, we have exploited no one. ³ I do not say this to condemn you; I have said before that you have such a place in our hearts that we would live or die with you. ⁴ I have spoken to you with great frankness; I take great pride in you.

When others don't share your intensity

Paul had many spiritual children, and they were all important to him. Despite their issues, he was proud of the Corinthians and would gladly die for them, making the problems in the relationship even more painful to him. It may feel safer to close your heart and end the relationship, but it is ultimately less satisfying. Paul chose to be vulnerable and open his heart, honestly sharing with them, even though that might cause more conflict.

Unfortunately, Paul's intensity was not shared by the Corinthians. Out of sight, out of mind. Other, flashier, apostles were on the scene and seemed to offer more. Church was exciting and life was good. Instead of taking pride in Paul as their spiritual father, they felt ashamed of him. They didn't hate him. He just wasn't that important to them. They probably weren't even aware of how much pain he was experiencing. They felt that Paul, in his intensity, had blown their misunderstandings out of proportion. Indeed, it turned out that his fears were unjustified.

The same thing can happen in a marriage. A wife at home with the children may focus her attention and affection on the family, while her husband is busy with work, travel, and enjoying the world's acclaim. In comparison, his wife and her concerns seem less important. Or it could be a man longing for a wife who has all but forgotten him with her focus on her family and friends, children, or career. In both cases, it's easy to lose perspective, and fear that the relationship is over.

At times someone's heart may be closed because we have broken faith and abused their trust. But Paul has been exemplary in his dealings with the Corinthians. He and his companions have:

- Wronged no one (never hurt a soul)

- Corrupted (betrayed, led astray) no one
- Exploited (cheated, taken advantage of) no one

Can you say the same of your ministry and relationships? Paul implies that the false apostles may have done all three. Perhaps you have been wounded by someone in ministry who exploited or took advantage of you. Maybe you were betrayed or corrupted by a man you looked up to, or have been wronged, and find it hard to forgive or trust anyone. Countless believers have left the church because of these bad experiences. Make sure God doesn't call you to account for harming his body.

Fears within, conflicts without

⁴I am greatly encouraged; in all our troubles my joy knows no bounds. ⁵ For when we came into Macedonia, we had no rest, but we were harassed at every turn—conflicts on the outside, fears within. ⁶ But God, who comforts the downcast, comforted us by the coming of Titus, ⁷ and not only by his coming but also by the comfort you had given him. He told us about your longing for me, your deep sorrow, your ardent concern for me, so that my joy was greater than ever.

This letter provides overwhelming evidence that being a great person of faith does not necessarily mean a trouble-free, happy life. Jesus was a man of sorrows and acquainted with grief. Paul was harassed at every turn (AMP: *oppressed in every way and afflicted at every turn*). Both were clearly in God's will and working for his glory. God had called Paul and his companions to Macedonia, but life was full of trouble. Instead of the rest Jesus promised, there were conflicts all around them, and fears within. We know fear is not of God, and his perfect love casts out fear. But don't feel guilty if you wrestle with fear, as though there is something wrong with you or your faith. Apparently it's not uncommon for mature Christians to experience fear. And Paul wasn't exactly experiencing the joy of the Lord. He was downcast. Yet somehow he is greatly encouraged. As he shared in chapter one, God comforts us, often through the comfort others have received. In this case it was from being reunited with a beloved brother and receiving good news about the very people he had been agonizing over. Nothing appears to have changed in his circumstances, but that fellowship and encouraging message gave Paul great joy – boundless joy. Sometimes when life is especially difficult, little blessings can bring greater joy than the good times.

Comfort and joy from relationships

We read in chapter two of Paul's distress at not finding Titus at Troas. This brother was obviously very dear to Paul, and having him come now was enough to significantly lift his spirits. Even better, Titus brought good news. Instead of mistreating Titus, as Paul had feared, the Corinthians had comforted him, assured him of their great concern and love for Paul, and expressed sorrow over the issues that had caused problems. In the days before cell phones and Emails it could take months to get this news. If you have anxiously waited a couple hours for news about a loved one, you can imagine how Paul felt waiting weeks or months. Waiting forces us to trust in God and give the situation to him!

Chapter 13 The Value of Relationships

The comfort and joy Paul received from relationships with beloved brothers and sisters were enough to get him through hard times. Do you have those kind of relationships? Too many Christians today are out of fellowship. Television and the internet can't substitute for real life relationships, which are worth investing in and fighting for, even though they can be painful.

Do you need to assure someone you're OK with them? Are you aware that pastors and other Christian leaders may be in need of comfort and encouragement? Could you be a Titus to a Paul? Are you experiencing conflicts without and fears within? Can you draw strength from brothers and sisters that will help you through them?

Chapter 14   Regrets
2 Corinthians 7:8-16

⁸ Even if I caused you sorrow by my letter, I do not regret it. Though I did regret it—I see that my letter hurt you, but only for a little while— ⁹ yet now I am happy, not because you were made sorry, but because your sorrow led you to repentance. For you became sorrowful as God intended and so were not harmed in any way by us. ¹⁰ Godly sorrow brings repentance that leads to salvation and leaves no regret, but worldly sorrow brings death.

Regrets. Do you have any? I think we all do. How many times have you said something hastily and damaged a relationship, only to regret it later? Paul felt that way. He had written the Corinthians a "painful" letter, and felt bad when he found out how much it hurt them. Did your dad ever tell you, "This hurts me more than it hurts you" as he was spanking you? As a kid I thought that was ridiculous. Now, as a father, I understand how hard it can be to hurt a child you love. But we trust it is for their good, as Paul found to be true with his painful letter.

Two very different reactions are possible when someone is confronted with their sin.

Worldly sorrow

The first reaction is to feel bad – perhaps sinking into depression and bitterness. But you don't bother doing anything about it. I have seen many inmates respond to God's correction with worldly sorrow - that melancholy mixture of self-pity and self-disgust called remorse. They feel bad about the consequences of their sin (getting arrested and incarcerated), but not the offense to God or the hurt caused others. Worldly sorrow doesn't last, and it produces no change. The man who follows this path will have many regrets. Too often I have gotten news of someone dying after they got out of prison, because there was no genuine repentance. They never truly died to self and got serious about forsaking sin. They were powerless to resist the world's temptations. Indeed, Paul says worldly sorrow always ends in death, since it never addresses the sin.

As you share with people, watch for worldly sorrow. Pray for them and warn them of its dangers. Never give the false impression they are doing right, when you – and, more importantly, God – can see right through them. We can unwittingly encourage worldly sorrow by neglecting to preach the need for true repentance, minimizing sin, or making excuses for continued rebellion. A man-centered gospel focused on what God can do for you may foster religious activity, but no real conversion. We need to preach God's holiness and the cost of discipleship.

Godly sorrow

In stark contrast, Godly sorrow is true brokenness and genuine repentance. In desperation you throw yourself on God's mercy and find forgiveness and a new start. Hatred for sin, and a determination to change, lead to salvation, new birth, and a life free of regrets.

Fostering Godly sorrow may not feel good or be popular, but don't stop calling people to genuine repentance. Brokenness isn't pleasant, but it is often necessary to bring about real change. Better to regret being a little too hard on someone, than seeing that person in a coffin and regretting a ministry that produced only worldly sorrow. We have been permissive with children – and reaped a terrible harvest. It's not easy, but don't back off disciplining your children. Don't let the excessive punishment often given in the past discourage you from appropriate consequences for rebellion and disobedience.

In your daily life and relationships, try to live so you have no regrets.

[11] *See what this godly sorrow has produced in you: what earnestness, what eagerness to clear yourselves, what indignation, what alarm, what longing, what concern, what readiness to see justice done. At every point you have proved yourselves to be innocent in this matter.* [12] *So even though I wrote to you, it was neither on account of the one who did the wrong nor on account of the injured party, but rather that before God you could see for yourselves how devoted to us you are.* [13] *By all this we are encouraged.*

It may have been a painful letter, but in the end Paul is encouraged. The letter gave the Corinthians a chance to show how devoted they were to Paul by their response to his correction.

Signs of genuine repentance

- Earnestness (deep sincerity or seriousness). They didn't take the problem lightly.
- Eagerness to clear themselves and regain Paul's approval.
- Indignation (anger – probably with the sinner - caused by something that is unfair or wrong).
- Alarm (at the serious consequences of allowing sin to continue). Better translated "a reverential fear" - of God, and of Paul as his servant.
- Longing (to have things right with Paul and the Lord).
- Concern (for the sinner, their church, and Paul).
- Readiness to see justice done by dealing appropriately with the offending parties.

Having made every effort to rectify past wrongs, they have proven themselves innocent. Things were not as bad as Paul feared.

[13] In addition to our own encouragement, we were especially delighted to see how happy Titus was, because his spirit has been refreshed by all of you. [14] I had boasted to him about you, and you have not embarrassed me. But just as everything we said to you was true, so our boasting about you to Titus has proved to be true as well. [15] And his affection for you is all the greater when he remembers that you were all obedient, receiving him with fear and trembling. [16] I am glad I can have complete confidence in you.

When a church responds to the Lord, it encourages pastors and other leaders. Paul was particularly grateful for the way they treated Titus. Titus had expected a difficult time, but left the Corinthians with his spirit refreshed. I observed that countless times with volunteers who cautiously came into the prison to minister to the inmates - and left with their spirits refreshed by the sincere believers there.

Like a father, Paul had boasted about the Corinthians, but was far from certain they would measure up to his hype. It can be tempting to talk about people who have mistreated you. It is sad to see a pastor bad-mouthing his congregation to another pastor. Part of love is always believing the best about people. Paul didn't poison Titus' mind with negativity toward the Corinthians, and it allowed Titus to go with an open heart.

Paul was afraid they might not receive Titus at all, but they received him with fear and respect – and love. Part of genuine repentance is obedience, and when Titus saw their tender hearts and willingness to obey he grew very fond of them.

"I am glad I can have complete confidence in you."

In a sense, this verse (16) summarizes the entire letter up to this point. The next two chapters will be devoted to the offering Paul is collecting, and the final three chapters also form a distinct unit. Despite all the struggles with this church, Paul has come to have complete confidence in them, like a father affirming his trust and confidence in his son despite the boy's earlier misdeeds. It is what a sincere believer longs to hear from his pastor, and from the Lord. It builds up the Corinthians, while preparing them for his request of an offering.

How do you receive someone God sends you? Do you make it your aim to refresh others' spirits? Do you delight your pastor and make him proud by your responsiveness to teaching and correction? Can those over you have complete confidence in you? Do you have complete confidence in those you are responsible for?

Chapter 15 Generous Giving
2 Corinthians 8:1-24

This was a headline story on Yahoo! in June of 2013:

Americans are giving less money to God

In the world of charitable giving, your alma mater may be faring better than your maker. While Americans are becoming more giving, a new study finds that fewer and fewer of their donations are going to houses of worship.

Paul has a word the church needs to hear in these next two chapters, both of which deal with offerings:

¹And now, brothers and sisters, we want you to know about the grace that God has given the Macedonian churches. ² In the midst of a very severe trial, their overflowing joy and their extreme poverty welled up in rich generosity. ³ For I testify that they gave as much as they were able, and even beyond their ability. Entirely on their own, ⁴ they urgently pleaded with us for the privilege of sharing in this service to the Lord's people. ⁵ And they exceeded our expectations: They gave themselves first of all to the Lord, and then by the will of God also to us. ⁶ So we urged Titus, just as he had earlier made a beginning, to bring also to completion this act of grace on your part. ⁷ But since you excel in everything—in faith, in speech, in knowledge, in complete earnestness and in the love we have kindled in you—see that you also excel in this grace of giving.

Christians in other places are giving more while we're giving less

The Corinthians, much like Americans, took pride in their spirituality and success as a church, so Paul gently prods them: Since you claim to excel in everything, make sure you excel in this matter of giving as well. Nothing like a little friendly competition to spur people to give!

Since Paul is writing from Macedonia, he has first-hand knowledge of their situation:

- The Macedonians are extremely poor and in the midst of a severe trial. Aside from persecution for their faith, the province had been ravaged by civil war and stripped of natural resources by the Romans.
- Despite the trial, they are overflowing with joy - and somehow that joy, combined with their poverty, led to great generosity.
- They gave until it hurt – going beyond what they might have been expected to give.
- There was no arm-twisting – they urgently pleaded for the privilege of giving. Perhaps Paul had hesitated to ask them since he was well aware of their poverty.
- They had giving, open hearts – to the Lord, to Paul and his companions, and now to the brothers in Jerusalem.

Their example provides a great challenge for the wealthy, comfortable, Corinthians.

Christians in other parts of the world put Americans to shame. If we are honest, most of us are so wealthy we don't feel any pain at all in our giving - but neither do we experience much of the joy of giving. I have been amazed at how readily and joyfully Christians in developing countries give to the Lord's work. Statistically, poor people give far more than the wealthy. Maybe that's why they're poor! The lowest income group in the US gives 4.3% of their income, while the wealthiest group gives 2.1% (http://www.mcclatchydc.com/news/politics-government/article24538864.html). When you have more, there is a perverse tendency to hoard, out of fear that you could actually end up in need. The Yahoo! article mentioned the 2008 recession as one reason giving was down, but the Macedonians were in an economic crisis and their giving was up!

Money is always a touchy subject

Personally, I don't like feeling pressured to give, and will run the other way if I sense manipulation. But I am eager to help a legitimate need. I have found most people feel that way. They're willing to give if two simple provisions are met:

The need is legitimate. One task of church leadership is to identify legitimate needs and make them known to the church. While giving to your local church should be your first priority, there are many other worthy causes. Paul knew the need of the Jerusalem church was urgent, and this offering had his 100% support. It was the mother church, in the holy city where Jesus ministered and was crucified. The church there had suffered famine and persecution. Support from gentile believers across the empire was an important demonstration of unity with their Jewish brothers.

Assure people their money will be handled with integrity. If I know the need is legitimate and the money will be used properly, I will be motivated to give. We have all heard of mismanaged offerings. You have the right to know where your money is going and should expect full integrity. I recently read that the president of a well-known Christian development and relief organization makes almost half a million dollars (http://www.forbes.com/top-charities). I have a hard time justifying that. Do your homework and find out where your donations are actually going. Pray about where to give. And be aware of emotional appeals or pressure to give.

As their spiritual father, Paul hopes the Corinthians can trust his judgment. He is wise enough to designate Titus as the one who will collect the gift, since Titus had developed a good relationship with them. Paul would not get a penny.

Giving is a grace

Three times in seven verses Paul uses the word grace. God's grace, which he gives freely, expecting nothing in return, enabled the Macedonian churches to respond so generously. We should offer others the same grace we have received from God. The Macedonians' gift was an act of grace, not based on merit, and with no expectation of anything in return.

Give until it hurts

Every Christian should be challenged to give according to their ability, in proportion to their income. The tithe is a good start. The test of faith is to trust God and give beyond your ability. Average giving to churches in the US was 2.3% in 2011 (http://www.religionnews.com/2013/10/24/report-church-giving-reaches-depression-era-record-lows). Massive advances in missions and Christian service would be possible if everyone tithed, to say nothing of giving until it hurt.

Do you see giving as a privilege? Have you ever pleaded with someone to let you give them money? Can you imagine how delighted pastors would be with that? It's a blessing to be in a position to give. I pray more people would beg to do so!

[8] I am not commanding you, but I want to test the sincerity of your love by comparing it with the earnestness of others. [9] For you know the grace of our Lord Jesus Christ, that though he was rich, yet for your sake he became poor, so that you through his poverty might become rich.

Make generosity your goal

God is a giver, and generosity should be a mark of the Christian. Look for every opportunity to give. Model generosity and teach it to your family. Not just with money, but with everything God has entrusted to you. We are God's stewards – responsible to use his gifts wisely for the benefit of his kingdom. Chances are if he sees that you have a giving heart he will give you more, to share with others.

Jesus is the ultimate example of generosity. He gladly let go of everything he had –ending his life with only his seamless robe (John 19:23). You could argue he was God and knew he was going back to the riches of heaven. But he called many wealthy people to give away everything they had to follow him.

Is God testing the sincerity of your love?

Paul knew that money is a great test of the sincerity of our love, and he was open about his plans to compare the Corinthians' sincerity with others, particularly the Macedonians. It is one thing to tell a brother in church you love him – it's a totally different matter to really help him when he loses his job or house. How would you feel giving all your money to a poor family so they could be rich - and you end up being poor? Or maybe giving your house to that family? That might be extreme, and God probably won't call many to do it, but money and possessions are not ours to hold on to. How sincere is your love? James writes: *Suppose a brother or a sister is without clothes and daily food. If one of you says to them, "Go in peace; keep warm and well fed," but does nothing about their physical needs, what good is it?* (James 2:15-16)

Have you even considered the possibility that God might call you to poverty?

[10] And here is my judgment about what is best for you in this matter. Last year you were the first not only to give but also to have the desire to do so. [11] Now finish the work, so that your eager willingness to do it may be matched by your completion of it, according to your means. [12] For if the

willingness is there, the gift is acceptable according to what one has, not according to what one does not have.

Are you willing?

The first step to faithful giving is your willingness, not how much you have or what you give. If you have a willing, generous heart, the rest will come naturally. If you are unable to give much, don't feel bad. Remember the widow's mite (Mark 12:41-44)? Give according to your means. God knows your heart. Are you holding back, or truly doing all you can?

Americans have a great history of giving to the church and missions. Yahoo! reported that our current giving is not measuring up to that history, and indeed it projects continuing declines in support of Christian ministry. Paul wants to make sure the Corinthians at least match their original gift. The previous year they had been the first to express interest in giving, and were the first to give. There had been problems in the church and their relationship with Paul which delayed the offering, but now things were better and it was time to move ahead. Maybe you had to cut back on giving due to a job loss or other financial problems, but now things are easing up and the Lord is urging you to be more generous. As a nation, if Christians got serious about giving we could have a huge impact for Christ.

Make it a point this week to cultivate generosity, to give until it hurts, and eagerly look for every opportunity to give. God deserves to fare better than your alma mater.

¹³ Our desire is not that others might be relieved while you are hard pressed, but that there might be equality. ¹⁴ At the present time your plenty will supply what they need, so that in turn their plenty will supply what you need. The goal is equality, ¹⁵ as it is written: "The one who gathered much did not have too much, and the one who gathered little did not have too little."

The goal is equality

That sounds good and seems quite simple. If we are all one in Christ and truly love each other, we will give what we can to someone in need. But for many Americans raised on free enterprise, capitalism, and rugged individualism, the goal of equality smacks too much of communism or socialism. That is very different from what Paul is teaching! Communism is forced on people by a secular government. Paul's teaching is completely voluntary, coming from a heart of love for God and others, and seeking equality among believers. Though we must be concerned for those outside the church, God's promise of provision - and command to equally distribute wealth - applies to the church. *Therefore, as we have opportunity, let us do good to all people, especially to those who belong to the family of believers* (Galatians 6:10).

This seems to answer the question raised in verse nine: Are we supposed to follow Christ's example and become poor so others can become rich? God might call you to do that, but generally the goal is to equalize things, not give so much that you are hurting. My concern is the gross inequality between Christians in wealthy countries and those living on a few dollars a day. There is no equality in the Body of Christ, even within the United States.

We're not talking about handouts, though. The assumption, as seen in verse fifteen, is that everyone is working. Scripture never endorses the idea of some lazy folks living off those who are hard-working. In our government programs we need to avoid encouraging irresponsibility. But if we have had the privilege of being born in a wealthy country and receiving a good education, it's wrong to hold onto what we have when hard-working brothers are barely getting by. At the moment, the Corinthians were doing well and the believers in Jerusalem were suffering. If Corinth were to experience a recession, that church could expect other Christians to come to its aid. For centuries the church practiced this kind of charity, preaching against greed and excess, while encouraging hard work. Today the preaching of prosperity has become a thin veil for greed. The motivation in giving has become "sowing," with the expectation that you'll get more back.

When we are obedient to God's command to give, and one part of the body helps the other, we can trust he will provide enough for all his people. Abundant provision is not given so some can live the good life while others are struggling. Our example is the Jews' experience with manna in the wilderness:

> *This is what the Lord has commanded: 'Everyone is to gather as much as they need. Take an omer for each person you have in your tent.'" The Israelites did as they were told; some gathered much, some little. And*

> when they measured it by the omer, the one who gathered much did not have too much, and the one who gathered little did not have too little. Everyone had gathered just as much as they needed. Then Moses said to them, "No one is to keep any of it until morning." However, some of them paid no attention to Moses; they kept part of it until morning, but it was full of maggots and began to smell. So Moses was angry with them. (Exodus 16:16-20)

What does this passage teach?
- Gather only what you need. Don't be greedy.
- If no one is greedy, God makes sure there's enough for everyone.
- You can't store it for the future. Trust God for your daily bread.

Don't try to set up a "manna savings account." Charles Hodge wrote in his commentary:

> If anyone attempted to hoard his portion, it spoiled in his hands. The lesson taught in Exodus and by Paul is that among the people of God the superabundance of one should be employed in relieving the necessities of others; any attempt to countervail this law will result in shame and loss. Property is like manna, it will not bear hoarding.

I learned this the hard way many years ago. I had an old Ford Pinto I wasn't using, and a brother in need of a car asked if he could borrow it. For a reason that I don't even remember, I made up a bogus excuse (lied) and told him no. The car had been running well, but when I went to drive it a little later the transmission died and it went straight to the junkyard. Somehow I am confident it would have run just fine for that brother.

^{16} Thanks be to God, who put into the heart of Titus the same concern I have for you. ^{17} For Titus not only welcomed our appeal, but he is coming to you with much enthusiasm and on his own initiative. ^{18} And we are sending along with him the brother who is praised by all the churches for his service to the gospel. ^{19} What is more, he was chosen by the churches to accompany us as we carry the offering, which we administer in order to honor the Lord himself and to show our eagerness to help. ^{20} We want to avoid any criticism of the way we administer this liberal gift. ^{21} For we are taking pains to do what is right, not only in the eyes of the Lord but also in the eyes of man.

^{22} In addition, we are sending with them our brother who has often proved to us in many ways that he is zealous, and now even more so because of his great confidence in you. ^{23} As for Titus, he is my partner and co-worker among you; as for our brothers, they are representatives of the churches and an honor to Christ. ^{24} Therefore show these men the proof of your love and the reason for our pride in you, so that the churches can see it.

How encouraging to know that a man of Paul's influence is personally concerned for you and your church (verse 16)! Alternate translations for "concern" are "zeal, care, and enthusiasm." It's wonderful to have someone enthusiastic about you, and to know God puts that kind of zeal for you in others' hearts! Even better, *God* has that concern, zeal, and enthusiasm for you! Has God given you enthusiasm for another church? Concern for other believers? What are you doing about it? Acting on this kind of God-given concern is essential to the healthy functioning of the Body of Christ.

Things specific to this collection

- Titus is the point man to receive the offering. He and Paul are partners and co-workers, united in spirit and sharing the same God-given concern for the Corinthians and this offering. He had become close to them, and is enthusiastic about the collection. Paul didn't pressure Titus to go – he took the initiative.
- A second, unnamed brother (often thought to be Luke or Barnabas), will come with Titus, further ensuring the integrity of the collection. He also was highly regarded by all the churches, and was chosen by them, not Paul.
- A third brother, also unnamed, will complete the team. Paul was showing the importance of the collection by sending top-notch ministers to receive it. An interesting note on verse 23: the Greek says *apostles* of the churches, suggesting there was a recognized body of apostles at that time.
- A little psychology: Paul calls their gift "liberal", perhaps in faith, or using the power of suggestion. He's doing everything he can to make sure it really

is liberal! He follows that up by portraying the offering as:
- A proof of their love ("If you don't give, you don't really love us; put your love into action").
- An opportunity to show others why he is so proud of them (like a parent wants his child to come through for other family members).
- A chance to show all the churches just how good they are.

Universal guidelines when dealing with money

- Take pains to do what is right, particularly in God's eyes, but also in the eyes of the world. How sad that Christians tend to be portrayed in the media as charlatans, abusing other peoples' money! Even worse, there's some foundation for that portrayal.
- Be aware that people are quick to criticize anything not done right. Endeavor to handle money with such integrity that you are above criticism.
- Proper handling of money honors and glorifies the Lord; improper handling dishonors him and brings disrepute to his name.

Some of the greatest leaders in the early church dedicated significant time and energy to this collection. Paul committed his best men, and months of their time, to delivering it. He was well aware of his accountability to God, and made every effort to assure it was handled with utmost integrity. Does economic assistance to struggling churches occupy the same priority in our ministries today? Or do we tend to tack it on as an option, after the really important matter of money for our own church and ministry? Are you willing to preach what the Bible says about financial equality among believers? Do you leave yourself open to criticism in your handling of finances? Is there something you could do in your church to bring it more in line with Paul's example? Are you seeking God and being obedient in your own giving?

Chapter 16 Freedom from Shame
2 Corinthians 9:1-4

One of my most vivid childhood memories is my father saying "shame" to my dog. Not in a loud voice, but one dripping with what to me felt like hatred. My poor dog would melt when she heard it, and I did too, because I was sure my dad felt that way about me. Have you experienced shame? In these few verses Paul shares his concern about being ashamed – and gives us the opportunity to look more closely at shame and how it affects us.

Making sure they are ready to give

[1] There is no need for me to write to you about this service to the Lord's people.

I have to chuckle at Paul sometimes. If there were no need for him to write them about this offering, why is he devoting two chapters of his letter to it?

[2] For I know your eagerness to help, and I have been boasting about it to the Macedonians, telling them that since last year you in Achaia were ready to give; and your enthusiasm has stirred most of them to action.

Whether it be giving, witnessing, or some other aspect of the Christian life, we need encouraging testimonies to spur us to action. Even if it is tinged with a competitive spirit, God will use it to accomplish his purposes.

- Is there something about your life or church that would be encouraging to others?
- Have you ever thanked someone whose example prompted you to greater obedience and deeper discipleship?
- Is there an inspiring story about God's work in another church you could share with your congregation to get them moving?

³But I am sending the brothers in order that our boasting about you in this matter should not prove hollow, but that you may be ready, as I said you would be.

There is nothing worse than talking about how great some brother or church is, only to be let down by them. Paul was sending this team of brothers to make sure that did not happen. Part of the discernment of a spiritual father or church overseer is knowing when to send in help, and who to send.

⁴For if any Macedonians come with me and find you unprepared, we—not to say anything about you—would be ashamed of having been so confident.

As an extra incentive, Paul drops word that some Macedonians may be joining him. Like the pressure to clean your house when important visitors are coming, this should motivate them to make sure everything is in order. If the Corinthians are not prepared, both them and Paul may be ashamed. Paul wants to spare himself from that, and avoid embarrassment for the Corinthians.

Chapter 16 Freedom from Shame

What is shame?

Shame is defined as "a painful feeling of humiliating disgrace, disrepute, or distress caused by guilt, shortcoming, impropriety, or the consciousness of wrong or foolish behavior." The root of the English word means "to cover or hide after being exposed - especially unexpected exposure of intimate aspects of yourself." (Oxford Dictionary) Shame is a wound to your self-esteem. It can involve a failure to reach your goals or ideals, and is associated with feelings of inferiority.

Shame in the Scriptures

Shame is powerful. God never intended us to experience it. *Adam and his wife were both naked, and they felt no shame* (Genesis 2:25). They only felt shame when they sinned, and then did what we usually do – covered themselves.

- Shame generally is the result of sin – ours or someone else's. *"We and our kings, our princes and our ancestors are covered with shame, Lord, because we have sinned against you"* (Daniel 9:8).
- Feeling shame for sin can be good if it drives you to repentance: *"Are they ashamed of their detestable conduct? No, they have no shame at all; they do not even know how to blush. So they will fall among the fallen; they will be brought down when I punish them," says the Lord"* (Jeremiah 6:15).
- There may be times when we need to make those in our care feel shame, as Paul did: *"I say this to shame you. Is it possible that there is nobody among you*

wise enough to judge a dispute between believers?" (1 Corinthians 6:5)

The Psalms frequently implore God to deliver us from shame and bring shame on our enemies.

- God promises you will not be put to shame if you trust in him: "*To you they cried out and were saved; in you they trusted and were not put to shame*" (Psalm 22:5).
- "*No one who hopes in you will ever be put to shame, but shame will come on those who are treacherous without cause*" (Psalm 25:3).
- The opposite of shame is honor: "*The wise inherit honor, but fools get only shame*" (Proverbs 3:35).

Shame is connected with fear, but God promises deliverance from past shame as well as the fear of shame in the future:

- "*Do not be afraid; you will not be put to shame. Do not fear disgrace; you will not be humiliated. You will forget the shame of your youth and remember no more the reproach of your widowhood*" (Isaiah 54:4).
- "*As it is written: 'See, I lay in Zion a stone that causes people to stumble and a rock that makes them fall, and the one who believes in him will never be put to shame'*" (Romans 9:33).

Even Christians face things that typically produce shame. Jesus did. The cross was the most shameful way to die, but: "*For the joy set before him he endured the cross, scorning its shame, and sat down at the right hand of the throne of*

Chapter 16 Freedom from Shame

God. Consider him who endured such opposition from sinners, so that you will not grow weary and lose heart" (Hebrews 12:2-3). Follow his example and keep your eyes on the Lord, scorning shame.

It's common to feel shame over something you cannot control. Look carefully at where the feelings of shame are coming from and be aware the devil will use those feelings to bring you down. In that case, renounce it, and rejoice that Jesus has taken away your shame! Unfortunately, we often bring shame on ourselves: *"The righteous hate what is false, but the wicked make themselves a stench and bring shame on themselves"* (Proverbs 13:5). If you want to avoid shame, pay attention to correction: *"Whoever disregards discipline comes to poverty and shame, but whoever heeds correction is honored"* (Proverbs 13:18).

Freedom from shame!

Paul was going out of his way to make sure he was not ashamed of the Corinthians when visitors arrived. Have you ever felt ashamed of your children when you had company and they acted out? Or of a church you were pastoring when you had some important visitor? As someone in authority, Paul had the right and the responsibility to work with the Corinthians to spare himself shame. As the authority in your home you have that same right and responsibility. Examine your life and your church to see if there is anything which could bring shame to you, your family, or your church. Then do what is necessary to put things in order.

Are there things in your past you feel ashamed of? Are there people in your life who try to make you feel ashamed, maybe even using it as a weapon against you? If you have not asked God's forgiveness, start there. If you are still involved in things that you are ashamed of, repent, and make the necessary changes. God wants to deliver you from shame. Spend time before him, letting go of that weight, giving him whatever has caused you shame, and rejoicing in his freedom.

Chapter 17 Sowing and Reaping
2 Corinthians 9:5-15

⁵ So I thought it necessary to urge the brothers to visit you in advance and finish the arrangements for the generous gift you had promised. Then it will be ready as a generous gift, not as one grudgingly given. ⁶ Remember this: Whoever sows sparingly will also reap sparingly, and whoever sows generously will also reap generously. ⁷ Each of you should give what you have decided in your heart to give, not reluctantly or under compulsion, for God loves a cheerful giver. ⁸ And God is able to bless you abundantly, so that in all things at all times, having all that you need, you will abound in every good work. ⁹ As it is written:

*"They have freely scattered their gifts to the poor;
  their righteousness endures forever."*

¹⁰ Now he who supplies seed to the sower and bread for food will also supply and increase your store of seed and will enlarge the harvest of your righteousness. ¹¹ You will be enriched in every way so that you can be generous on every occasion, and through us your generosity will result in thanksgiving to God.

Did you notice what word occurs six times in these few short verses? Generous! We talked about generosity and its importance for Christian growth in chapter 15. It should be a natural result of knowing Jesus as you reflect his giving heart.

They already promised to be generous – but sometimes we need a little extra encouragement to follow through on the promises we make. Have you ever been touched by an appeal for money, only to later regret your promise to give?

Extortion!

Paul knew money could be given grudgingly. He uses the words *"reluctantly"* and *"under compulsion"* to describe that sinful heart attitude. It's an attitude that is legalistic, betrays a selfish heart, and displeases God. The Amplified Version calls it *"extortion"*: wringing money out of donors. Have you ever felt extorted in church, like someone was trying to wring money out of you? What you give should not be determined by outside pressure. Prayerfully make your decision and then follow through on it. Your decision is between you and God. He wants to give you a heart that joyfully looks for opportunities to share the abundance he's given you - or sacrifice of the little you have. Do you want to experience more of God's love? Develop a cheerful, giving, heart! He loves that!

Sowing and reaping

The principle of sowing and reaping is very popular today. While there is some truth in it, Paul never imagined it would be used to manipulate people to give out of the erroneous expectation that they would become rich. The self-centeredness often evident goes totally against God's purpose in giving you an abundant harvest. When he sees a sincere, generous heart that freely sows what he has given you, he will pour out more - so you can give more away. He promises all you *need* - anything beyond that is for works of righteousness; blessing others who have less. He enriches you so you can be generous, not so you can live a lavish lifestyle.

How does this reflect on God? The Lord's goodness is clearly seen and he is given thanks and praise. We want to make *God* look good in our giving, and direct any praise to *him*. If your motivation is wrong you can miss out on the blessing:

> *"Be careful not to practice your righteousness in front of others to be seen by them. If you do, you will have no reward from your Father in heaven. "So when you give to the needy, do not announce it with trumpets, as the hypocrites do in the synagogues and on the streets, to be honored by others. Truly I tell you, they have received their reward in full. But when you give to the needy, do not let your left hand know what your right hand is doing, so that your giving may be in secret. Then your Father, who sees what is done in secret, will reward you* (Matthew 6:1-4).

God knows what you're giving. There is no need to give to impress others.

[12] This service that you perform is not only supplying the needs of the Lord's people but is also overflowing in many expressions of thanks to God. [13] Because of the service by which you have proved yourselves, others will praise God for the obedience that accompanies your confession of the gospel of Christ, and for your generosity in sharing with them and with everyone else. [14] And in their prayers for you their

hearts will go out to you, because of the surpassing grace God has given you. ^{15} Thanks be to God for his indescribable gift!

The greatest giver

God has given more than you could ever possibly give! And every day he keeps giving you his grace!

- You can get to know his loving heart by sharing in the privilege and joy of supplying the needs of his people.
- Your giving is one way of proving the sincerity of your faith, which is shown by your obedience to God.
- The material blessing you may receive isn't the most important result of giving. Those who receive your gift may be motivated to pray for you, and then you will be spiritually blessed.

These chapters comprise the longest passage in the Bible on giving. Paul concludes it by pointing us back to the greatest giver of all, and the greatest gift: his Son. Far from being manipulative, Paul is trying to form a generous heart in these believers so they can experience the great joy of giving – and be blessed by the prayers of those who receive. He especially wants offerings of praise and thanksgiving to be lifted up to God.

How is your giving? What are you sowing into? What are you doing with the excess God gives you? Give it away instead of using it for unnecessary pleasures, and see how

Chapter 17 Sowing and Reaping

God blesses you. Challenge any reluctance you may feel, and take advantage of every opportunity to give!

Chapter 18 Weapons for the Battle
2 Corinthians 10:1-6

Paul ended his first letter to the Corinthians talking about the collection for the Jerusalem church. The two chapters we just finished also focus on that collection, and the last verse finishes with a triumphant: *"Thanks be to God for his indescribable gift!"* Was that actually the end of the letter? Many people believe so. These last four chapters (10-13) have a decidedly different tone. Many think this is all or part of the so-called "difficult letter" Paul referred to.

Timid or bold?

[1]By the humility and gentleness of Christ, I appeal to you—I, Paul, who am "timid" when face to face with you, but "bold" toward you when away!

Have you discovered that people talk a lot differently on Facebook, Twitter, or in a text message than they would face to face? When there is something difficult to communicate - like breaking up with a girlfriend - many find a text easier. Paul lived long before texting, but he had a reputation for being much bolder in letters than in person. Apparently his personal presence wasn't too impressive, and a certain timidity characterized him when he was actually with them.

The word translated "timid" could also be translated "lowly", or "humble." It has the negative connotation of being faint-hearted. Paul's opponents mockingly described him as timid, but bold in his letters, in the sense of a coward who acts tough – when no danger is present.

Meek and gentle

Given this perception, and the difficult task before him, it is surprising his appeal is to the *humility* and *gentleness* of Christ! Being strong and forceful doesn't mean you can't be humble! Nor does it mean you have to be abusive! There is a special strength in gentleness! Even though meekness and gentleness are not traits we typically associate with Paul, Christ has given him that spirit as he writes.

The word translated "humility" would be better translated "meekness." We rarely talk about meekness today. If we do, it is not in a positive light. And no wonder! The Free Dictionary defines meek as *"humbly patient or docile, as under provocation from others; overly submissive or compliant; spiritless; tame."* Yuck! An "obsolete" definition is *"gentle; kind."* Christ's meekness was evident in his submitting to the suffering of the cross. The meek Christian is not weak, but one who accepts God's discipline, knowing that God uses the abuse of evil men to chasten and purify us.

Gentleness is another quality not usually seen as masculine or desirable. The Free Dictionary defines it as *"kindly; amiable, not severe, rough, or violent; mild."* You might as well say gentleness is effeminate or wishy washy! What man wants to be like that? No wonder gentlemen seem in short supply today! Jesus displayed his gentleness, or kindness, in dealing with the woman caught in adultery (John 8:1-11). Paul is appealing to them by this meekness and gentleness.

It doesn't seem like a winning strategy, given the strength of his opposition, and particularly the spiritual battle he will describe momentarily. But perhaps we could accomplish more if we made our appeals in the same spirit!

² I beg you that when I come I may not have to be as bold as I expect to be toward some people who think that we live by the standards of this world.

I ask that when I am present I need not be bold with the confidence with which I propose to be courageous against some, who regard us as if we walked according to the flesh. (NASB)

Is that an empty threat? Is Paul hoping to avoid a difficult confrontation? Apparently the situation is bad, and Paul is prepared to do whatever is necessary to resolve it. He hopes the Corinthians respond to this letter so he can concentrate on building them up when he visits. The problem seems to be a small group which doesn't understand what being a Christian is all about. They are the ones in the flesh (the literal meaning of the Greek word), and dealing with the situation as worldly people would. What they don't realize is that Paul is in a whole different kingdom, where he is able to be humble and gentle - and strong.

Fight – but not like the world does

³ For though we live in the world, we do not wage war as the world does.

For though we walk in the flesh, we do not war according to the flesh. (NASB)

Warfare is part of life. There is no way to avoid it. As long as we are in this world there will be conflict with the kingdom of darkness. You cannot decide to get out of the world to avoid conflict, although some Christians attempt to. Instead you have to decide *how* you're going to fight. Do you remember how you used to fight before you knew Christ? Maybe no one ever told you, but that will not work anymore as a believer. If you wage war like the world does, in the flesh, you are going to find yourself exhausted and on the losing end most of the time.

Think back on some recent battles in your life. How did you fight?

[4] The weapons we fight with are not the weapons of the world. On the contrary, they have divine power to demolish strongholds.

For the weapons of our warfare are not of the flesh, but divinely powerful for the destruction of fortresses. (NASB)

The world's weapons

- Guns, knives, and other instruments of destruction.
- The courts.
- Slander; a war of words.
- Lies and deceit.
- Manipulation and propaganda.
- Human wisdom and philosophy.
- Psychology.
- Human cleverness and ingenuity.
- Organizing ability.

- Reliance on charm or forcefulness of personality.

Which of those was your weapon of choice in the past? Which have you used recently? You may temporarily win a battle with those weapons, but they never win the war. They never get at the real issue, because we are in a spiritual battle. *"For our struggle is not against flesh and blood, but against the rulers, against the authorities, against the powers of this dark world and against the spiritual forces of evil in the heavenly realms"* (Ephesians 6:12). Not many people – even Christians – see that. Zechariah 4:6 reminds us that battles are won *"'Not by might nor by power, but by my Spirit,' says the Lord Almighty."*

Strongholds

To prevail in this war we need weapons with divine power, which are available only to the believer. Unless we demolish strongholds we will find ourselves in constant skirmishes, but never winning the battle.

What is a stronghold? It's the only time this Greek word is used in the New Testament. Edgardo Silvoso defines it as *"A mind set impregnated with hopelessness that causes the believer to accept as unchangeable something that they know is contrary to the will of God."* I picture a fortress being built. Each time a sin is committed a brick gets set into the wall. When sin continues without repentance those "bricks" begin to build a stronghold. Eventually it becomes so much a part of your life that Satan has a grip on you in that area, and you need deliverance to get free, using those divine weapons.

- Nations, communities, and families become strongholds of demonic power when they repeatedly reject God and pursue evil. Satan then uses his evil forces to influence and control them.
- The headlong pursuit of our own foolish ideas results in ideological strongholds through which Satan influences culture and society, and dominates their world view.
- Peoples' sin, feelings, and behavior patterns result in personal strongholds.

Of course, to do battle you have to know who you are fighting. Most people have a number of strongholds in their lives, often dating back to childhood. They usually are unaware of them. They may think of them as weaknesses or part of their personality. You need spiritual discernment to identify them – and divine weapons to demolish them. Though exposure is a first step to victory, in itself it rarely demolishes a stronghold. Your best efforts and all the psychotherapy and twelve-step programs in the world won't work either.

Our weapons

- God's Word, the sword of the Spirit. Just as Jesus used appropriate Scriptures with the devil during his temptations, we need to know the Word so we can find the right Scripture and then proclaim it in faith and authority.
- Prayer, especially Spirit-directed prayer, and prayer in tongues if you have a prayer language. These are prayers of authority based on God's Word, which

you proclaim in Jesus' Name. They can include rebuking and renouncing the devil and his demons. I have found prayer that identifies and renounces each "brick" or sin that has built the stronghold in the person's life to be especially effective.
- Deliverance. God places people in his body with the gift and authority to bind and cast out any oppressive evil spirits. You certainly can pray for your own deliverance, but a tough stronghold may require others' prayers.
- Means of grace God has provided, like regular participation in a solid church, receiving anointed preaching of the Word, baptism, and the Lord's Supper.
- As you go into battle you will want to have on the spiritual armor described in Ephesians 6.
- Truth, faith, love, and a holy life can also serve as weapons.

[5] *We demolish arguments and every pretension that sets itself up against the knowledge of God* (AMP: *arguments and theories and reasonings and every proud and lofty thing that sets itself up against the [true] knowledge of God), and we take captive every thought to make it obedient to Christ.*

The battle

Paul is probably thinking of the situation in Corinth, but this gives a glimpse into the nature of the spiritual battle.

One key way the enemy wages war against the kingdom of God is keeping people ignorant of who God really is. Since our knowledge of God primarily comes from the Bible, that is usually accomplished through either misinterpreting it or keeping people from actually reading it.

Jesus is the other primary revelation of who God is. Popular portrayals of Christ in literature, pictures, and the media tend to focus on his teachings and loving personality, often to the exclusion of his sharp criticism of hypocrites and masterful way of handling conflict. We may see him more as a baby in the manger or a helpless man on the cross than the mighty warrior portrayed in Revelation.

Our world is full of arguments on lifestyle, how the world was created, and proper expressions of gender and sexuality. Though we can respond to those arguments with a clear presentation of God's truth, if we battle as the world does and get into debates, we will find ourselves losing. The only way to deal with those arguments is to destroy them. Challenge the lie, present the truth, and allow the Spirit of God to open peoples' minds.

The principle battlefield is your mind. While you may be able to control your actions, it is much harder to control your thoughts. When you start fighting fantasies, doubts, and temptations in the flesh you usually lose. Don't let those thoughts have free reign. Take them captive. Picture grabbing hold of wild, uncontrolled thoughts and taking them directly to Christ. Then allow him, as your Lord, to order them, so you can have his mind. Fill your thoughts with his Word, worship, and other positive, edifying things.

The path to victory in the battle of the mind is obedience. When you make a decision to obey the will of God as revealed in the Bible, you will find yourself defeating temptation, doubt, and fantasies. Disobedience opens a flood of perverse thoughts and fosters the growth of strongholds.

[6] And we will be ready to punish every act of disobedience, once your obedience is complete.

This is an odd verse. How would you feel about someone coming into your church to punish every act of disobedience? How would they know about them? What kind of punishment would be involved? Maybe putting them out of the fellowship or even handing them over to Satan, as in the discipline Paul described in 1 Corinthians. Who would mete out that punishment today? And if believers' obedience was complete, why would there be any need to punish disobedience? It appears Paul wants to give them every opportunity to obey. Only when every other means was exhausted would he have to deal with those who persisted in disobedience and held onto their strongholds. At that point we can assume his appeal would no longer be in the meekness and gentleness of Christ. He would boldly step forward to use the spiritual weapons Christ has entrusted to us:

> *"If they refuse to listen even to the church, treat them as you would a pagan or a tax collector. Truly I tell you, whatever you bind on earth will be bound in heaven, and whatever you loose on earth will be loosed in heaven"* (Matthew 18:17-18).

If those strongholds were allowed to remain in the church, they would weaken it and allow Satan a foothold to influence the whole body. God prefers to deal gently with us. Only when he has exhausted every means of getting us on track will he resort to harsher measures. But out of love and concern for his Body and Christ's reputation, he will do what is necessary. We are in a war, and he expects you to fight. He has given you the weapons and authority to do so. Now it's up to you to use them and take back what the devil has stolen. Paul is not about to sit back and let the devil have his way with this church. This letter is part of his warfare. Grab your weapons, and fight the good fight.

Chapter 19 The Lord's Work in the Lord's Way

2 Corinthians 10:7-18

Are you serious about doing the Lord's work in the Lord's way? This passage raises several serious questions about the way we do church!

1. Do not judge other ministries by appearances.

⁷ You are judging by appearances. If anyone is confident that they belong to Christ, they should consider again that we belong to Christ just as much as they do.

The New Living Translation starts verse seven, "*Look at the obvious facts.*" It is so easy to judge by outward appearances instead of looking at the heart – or at the facts! It is easy to be deceived! What you see may not be reality. The Corinthians are falling into the devil's trap of superficiality and ignoring what is really important. They compare Paul's unimpressive appearance with the "super apostles" who:

- Boasted of a great heritage (11:21-22)
- Had first-rate letters of reference (3:1-3)
- Claimed supernatural visionary experiences (12:1, 12)
- Were good speakers (10:10; 11:6)
- Were refined (11:6)
- Were assertive (11:20)

No wonder these false apostles were winning over the Corinthians and could even cast doubt on Paul's salvation! But instead of love they were sowing division and discord in the Body of Christ.

⁸ So even if I boast somewhat freely about the authority the Lord gave us for building you up rather than tearing you down, I will not be ashamed of it.

Don't be put off by Paul's repeated boasting. Since these other "apostles" were very free to boast and ridicule him, Paul also resorts to boasting to win the battle for the heart of the Corinthian church.

Here Paul identifies the foundation of apostleship: authority. He had authority because God sent him to Corinth and used him to establish the church there. God gave him that authority, and he would be sinning if he didn't exercise it. The other apostles did not have that God-given authority, but relied on human strategies (worldly weapons) to win the Corinthians' hearts.

2. Understand the critical role of authority in ministry

Godly authority, whether in a church or home, should not tear people down in a harsh or judgmental way. It should build them up. Paul has been stern with this church only because of the severity of their sin. His authority was based on the father-child relationship established when he planted the church. Do you have God-given authority because you are functioning in your calling? Does it come from birthing spiritual sons and daughters? Are you using that authority to build others up? Are you under someone with genuine authority? Are you being built up?

⁹ I do not want to seem to be trying to frighten you with my letters. ¹⁰ For some say, "His letters are weighty and forceful, but in person he is unimpressive and his speaking amounts to nothing."

Paul already admitted in verse one that physical presence and speech were not his strong points. Perhaps that was why he needs to be more forceful in his letters. His deep theological insights were expressed in those letters. Can you imagine not having a "weighty" letter like Romans?

¹¹ Such people should realize that what we are in our letters when we are absent, we will be in our actions when we are present.

Since the other apostles were in Corinth and Paul was not, those apostles may have implied Paul was unable to follow through on what he wrote. But they were wrong.

¹² We do not dare to classify or compare ourselves with some who commend themselves. When they measure themselves by themselves and compare themselves with themselves, they are not wise.

3. **There's a great need of valid recommendation for ministry**

"Commend" means "to represent as worthy, qualified, or desirable; to recommend." (Collins Dictionary) Traditionally such commendation was expressed in the church by ordination, where a recognized group of godly leaders endorsed a person as qualified for ministry, and recommended that person as a servant of the church. J. B. Phillips paraphrased this verse:

> *Of course we shouldn't dare include ourselves in the same class as those who write their own testimonials, or even to compare ourselves with them! All they are doing, of course, is to measure themselves by their own standards or by comparisons within their own circle, and that doesn't make for accurate estimation, you may be sure.*

The situation in Corinth was ridiculous! The false apostles couldn't even begin to compare with Paul! Instead of being commended by God and sent out by a church with apostolic authority, they promoted themselves! They were not willing to measure themselves by honest comparison with true apostles, or, more importantly, by God's standards.

Too many people in ministry today recommend themselves, unwilling to submit to time-honored standards for Christian ministry. Anyone can start a church or establish an internet presence. Little is known about their personal life or beliefs. They print their own testimonials, use their own standards to measure themselves, and compare themselves, usually by worldly guidelines of success, to others in their own circle.

If you are in ministry, who has recommended you? Do they have the legitimate authority to do so? Who commended those in authority over you?

*¹³ We, however, will not boast beyond proper limits, but will confine our boasting to the sphere of service (*NLT: *area of authority) God himself has assigned to us, a sphere that also includes you.*

4. Minister in your God-given area of authority

With all the competition at Corinth it would have been tempting to make extravagant boasts. If you have to defend yourself and your calling, be careful to do it within the area of authority God has given you.

This is an interesting concept: God assigns spheres of service. Literally, it means there are lines, a territory, which he marks out and then assigns to someone. It is our responsibility to learn where those lines are drawn and to stay within them. That is where your authority lies. If you step outside your assigned sphere you lose your authority - and may even be in someone else's territory. When a pastor invites you into his church you step into his sphere. Make sure you honor his authority and the ministry God has given him. If you attempt to intrude into another's sphere, or church, you are inviting all kinds of trouble. The same is true of your home. You have authority in your family, but be careful of stepping into another person's territory, or home!

¹⁴ We are not going too far in our boasting, as would be the case if we had not come to you, for we did get as far as you with the gospel of Christ. ¹⁵ Neither do we go beyond our limits by boasting of work done by others. Our hope is that, as your faith continues to grow, our sphere of activity among you will greatly expand, ¹⁶ so that we can preach the gospel in the regions beyond you. For we do not want to boast about work already done in someone else's territory.

Paul is keenly aware of the territory given a minister by the Lord. What a shame that competing churches show so little respect for that! If you are thinking of establishing a new church, find out if it is in another pastor's territory! If God has given that territory to him, even if you don't agree with everything he is doing, I would be very hesitant to establish a competing work.

God appears to break up geographical areas into territories which he then assigns to an apostle or pastor. How do we determine what that area is – and who is responsible for enforcing those boundaries? The Roman Catholic Church has followed what probably began in the first century church, dividing an area into "parishes." Perhaps we should pay more attention to that concept. Even Paul's detractors seemed to acknowledge that the group Paul established was the legitimate body for that area. They didn't simply start a competing church. If this is true, what a mess we're in today. There can be dozens of churches in a small area of a city! Some have suggested that Paul is referring to his "territory" as the gentiles in general, but there seem to be definite geographic boundaries in mind here. We need to seriously grapple with what Scripture says. If we are ignoring a basic principle of ministry, we may well be quenching the Spirit of God. Even worse, we are probably sinning.

5. Be open to expanding your territory

There *is* a place, however for godly ambition in expanding your territory. I think of the Prayer of Jabez *("Oh, that you would bless me and expand my territory! Please be with me in all that I do, and keep me from all trouble and pain!"*, 1 Chronicles 4:10). Paul echoes that desire to extend into new regions. Perhaps part of his urgency in getting the church straightened out was to enable the believers' faith to grow, thus allowing his sphere of activity among them to expand. He may have imagined overseeing teams from the church going into surrounding areas. I like the way John Calvin phrased what he felt Paul was saying here:

> "If you had progressed as far as you ought, I should by now be occupied in gaining new churches and I should have your assistance in doing so. But, as things are, you are delaying me by your weakness. Yet I hope that the Lord will grant you to make greater progress in the future, so that the glory of my ministry may be increased according to the measure of the calling of God."

Are there doors God may be opening for you to expand his work?

6. Do not take credit for another person's work

Paul also warns about taking credit for someone else's hard work. Imagine a ministry established after years of intense prayer and spiritual battle. Strongholds have been broken down and the area has been opened up to the gospel. Then someone else comes in and starts a new church there, claiming they have "brought the gospel" to a rough part of town. As a prison chaplain I used to grimace when ministries would come where I had been laboring for years and then publish glossy accounts of bringing the Gospel to this terrible prison. Most of the "conversions" cited were men who had already accepted Christ!

Are you careful to give credit where it is due, and not take credit for someone else's work?

[17] But, "Let the one who boasts boast in the Lord." [18] For it is not the one who commends himself who is approved, but the one whom the Lord commends.

At the end of the day, you must seek the Lord's approval for your work and be recommended by him, with confirmation by trustworthy servants who know you. All too many ministers are into self-commendation. Be careful of boasting about yourself and the great ministry you have! Our boast should always be in the Lord.

Chapter 20 The Masquerade
2 Corinthians 11:1-15

I find them annoying. You've probably seen a movie in which hideous aliens put on carefully crafted disguises that make them look like attractive men and women. At the appropriate moment they peel the mask off and you discover who they really are. It is a disguise, a deception. Things are not the way they seem. They are part of a "maskerade." In this passage we will learn that, like it or not, you are in a masquerade. My hope and prayer is that you will have the discernment to recognize the disguises – and that your spirituality isn't a mask for something more sinister.

[1] I hope you will put up with me in a little foolishness. Yes, please put up with me!

Paul just warned about self-commendation, so he's apologetic about his "foolishness." But in this masquerade it was necessary, to counteract the shameless false apostles who were rapidly winning over the Corinthians. Sometimes we have to assert ourselves more than feels comfortable, not to promote self, but to fight for our family or church.

Have a godly, fatherly, jealousy!

[2] I am jealous for you with a godly jealousy. I promised you to one husband, to Christ, so that I might present you as a pure virgin to him.

Don't let those you love get caught up in the masquerade! Paul's job as a spiritual father was not to hold onto the Corinthians for himself, but, like a father with his daughter, protect their purity and prepare them to be united to Christ. A charming man can sweep a girl off her feet, but he may be masquerading as a gentleman when all he wants is her body. Just as a father fights that man off, Paul will fight for his beloved spiritual children. Jealousy is not all bad! It is wholly appropriate to have a godly jealousy for your family, people you are discipling, or a church you are pastoring.

If you're in ministry, do you have a father's heart and jealousy for the purity and well-being of your church? Are you aware God is trusting you to prepare them to be united to Jesus? Only then will your job as spiritual father be finished.

Husband, Ephesians five speaks of your responsibility to present your wife to Christ as a spotless bride. It may feel strange to think about handing your wife over to Christ, but she won't be yours for eternity! Are you encouraging her purity of heart and love for Jesus?

Maintain your devotion to Christ

³But I am afraid that just as Eve was deceived by the serpent's cunning, your minds may somehow be led astray from your sincere and pure devotion to Christ.

The masquerade starts with a subtle shift in your relationship to Jesus. The serpent was successful in deceiving Eve and forever changing the husband/wife relationship. Continuing the thought of the church as

Christ's bride, Paul calls the Corinthians to have the pure devotion for Jesus that a woman should have for her husband. A woman about to get married is focused on her wedding and anticipating being with the man she loves. Is your love for Jesus wholehearted, pure, and undivided?

The false apostles, with devilish cunning, were subtly leading the Corinthians astray. It's usually not blatant. With Eve it was an innocent piece of fruit. Today it could be ministry. Success. Family. Money. The internet. All the programs in church. Paul says that their minds were led astray. What starts with our thoughts usually manifests itself later in actions. Marital unfaithfulness almost always starts in the mind. You are not exempt from Satan's deception! He is cunning! He still uses the same tactics today that were so successful with Eve. How could he be trying to lead you astray?

A different Jesus, a different spirit, a different gospel

[4] For if someone comes to you and preaches a Jesus other than the Jesus we preached, or if you receive a different spirit from the Spirit you received, or a different gospel from the one you accepted, you put up with it easily enough.

I have a hard time with pastors who criticize other churches and ministries, and I try to avoid doing so. Yet Paul doesn't hesitate to expose the disguises of demonic doctrines. Jesus freely exposed the hypocrisy of the Pharisees and warned people not to join their masquerade:

> *"Woe to you, teachers of the law and Pharisees, you hypocrites! You are like*

> *whitewashed tombs, which look beautiful on the outside but on the inside are full of the bones of the dead and everything unclean. In the same way, on the outside you appear to people as righteous but on the inside you are full of hypocrisy and wickedness."* (Matthew 23:27-28)

Frankly, I shudder at much of what passes for Christianity in America today. When I flip through religious TV channels I often feel like I'm observing a totally different religion.

There are many different christs! Do you preach the Jesus of the Gospels? Or a Jesus seen through 21st century American glasses? Many people pick and choose from what Jesus taught. The real Jesus said our righteousness must exceed that of the Pharisees (Matthew 5:20). He claimed exclusivity: *"No one comes to the Father but by me"* (John 14:6). Since these false apostles mocked Paul's weaknesses, they may have downplayed the cross and Christ's suffering, not unlike some today who imply that suffering is a sign of weak faith.

Here, in verse 4, Paul says it is possible to receive a different spirit, even after receiving the Holy Spirit! Have you ever considered that possibility – in yourself or in those you minister to? Corinth was a Spirit-filled church with many supernatural manifestations. If you embrace a lie, give yourself to a false expression of Christianity, or put on a mask and become part of the masquerade, you may receive a demonic spirit.

There are so many gospels today! The Full Gospel. The Prosperity Gospel. The Seeker-Friendly Gospel. The Emotionally Healthy Gospel. The Purpose Driven Gospel. I'm not saying all those are heresies, but there is a danger in becoming so focused on a gimmick or particular aspect of the faith that we are pulled away from our sincere devotion to Jesus. What seems to be left out of so many of these gospels is the heart of the true Gospel: Jesus Christ crucified and resurrected who offers justification, redemption, and salvation to those who genuinely repent and follow him as Lord.

Paul is troubled because the Corinthians are quick to accept whatever anyone offers them. We don't have to be police, but we must be vigilant of what comes into our churches and homes. It's possible to hear a solidly biblical sermon in church and then go home to watch a television preacher present a totally different gospel. Somehow we have to educate and alert the church to the dangers in these other gospels. We are not to tolerate them! Take a moment to evaluate the gospel you're hearing in your church, and the one you're following. Read the gospels again to be sure that you're following the real Jesus.

Don't be deceived by the disguises

⁵I do not think I am in the least inferior to those "super-apostles." ⁶I may indeed be untrained as a speaker, but I do have knowledge. We have made this perfectly clear to you in every way.

If it looks too good to be true, it probably is. God uses flawed vessels that display *his* power and glory. Be careful of the super slick pastor! Paul seemed inferior when compared to the other apostles. It seems odd that he would have to defend his knowledge, since he was educated by one of the top rabbis of the day (Acts 22:3). He did lack training as a speaker, and that, along with not being one of the Twelve, seemed to continually haunt him. Yet, as he frequently pointed out, God probably did that on purpose to keep him humble and focused on the message. Are you painfully aware of something that makes you feel inferior to others, whether in ministry or daily life? It can be hard to let go of that struggle, but God may have allowed it for a purpose. Don't let that feeling of inferiority keep you from what he has called you to do. When I see others, like men with no arms or legs, and the great things they're doing for the Lord, I'm convicted by the triviality of my own concerns.

Money is big in the masquerade!

⁷Was it a sin for me to lower myself in order to elevate you by preaching the gospel of God to you free of charge? ⁸I robbed other churches by receiving support from them so as to serve you. ⁹And when I was with you and needed something, I was not a burden to anyone, for the brothers who came from Macedonia supplied what I needed. I have kept myself from being a burden to you in any way, and will continue to do so.

This has come up repeatedly. The false apostles received liberal offerings from the Corinthians. In marked contrast, Paul took pride in never having asked for – or received – any money from them. His detractors twisted it to imply he really was not an apostle, since he had not asked for money.

What may have particularly rankled his opponents was the exposure of their own selfish motives in taking the Corinthians' money.

¹⁰ As surely as the truth of Christ is in me, nobody in the regions of Achaia will stop this boasting of mine. ¹¹ Why? Because I do not love you? God knows I do!

Paul was motivated by the need for the truth to be known and his love for the church. He could not bear the thought of letting people get lost in the masquerade. And you shouldn't either.

Satan masquerades as an angel of light

¹² And I will keep on doing what I am doing in order to cut the ground from under those who want an opportunity to be considered equal with us in the things they boast about. ¹³ For such people are false apostles, deceitful workers, masquerading as apostles of Christ. ¹⁴ And no wonder, for Satan himself masquerades as an angel of light. ¹⁵ It is not surprising, then, if his servants also masquerade as servants of righteousness. Their end will be what their actions deserve.

Paul knows that he's in a spiritual battle and so he must rip the masks off: these so-called apostles are servants of Satan! Were he to back off and give up he would be letting the devil win. I am sure he was prayerfully fighting this battle, but faith does not mean just sitting back and letting God take care of it. Paul will honorably fight for the church. You also may need to rip the masks off false doctrines and false teachers.

Satan is the father of lies and deceit is his modus operandi. He rarely goes around with a pitchfork and horns, and is probably far more present in the church than we care to imagine. Remember Jesus' parable of the wheat and tares (a useless species of rye-grass which resembles wheat until the ear appears)?

> *"The kingdom of heaven is like a man who sowed good seed in his field. But while everyone was sleeping, his enemy came and sowed weeds among the wheat, and went away. When the wheat sprouted and formed heads, then the weeds also appeared. The owner's servants came to him and said, 'Sir, didn't you sow good seed in your field? Where then did the weeds come from?' "'An enemy did this,' he replied. "The servants asked him, 'Do you want us to go and pull them up?' "'No,' he answered, 'because while you are pulling the weeds, you may uproot the wheat with them. Let both grow together until the harvest. At that time I will tell the harvesters: First collect the weeds and tie them in bundles to be burned; then gather the wheat and bring it into my barn.'"*
> (Matthew 13:24-30)

Demons are not the only ones doing Satan's bidding. He has a host of men and women in this masquerade who look like "servants of righteousness." The church today is full of them, along with false apostles and deceitful workers. Jesus said *"Many false prophets will appear and deceive many people... the love of most will grow cold. For false Christs and false prophets will appear and perform great signs and wonders to deceive, if possible, even the elect."* (Matthew 24:11, 12, 24) Is the church aware of it? Do pastors and other leaders realize how serious the threat is? Do they even consider the possibility that some of their leaders might be part of the masquerade?

Even you may have been deceived, following a false apostle, embracing another gospel, and looking like a servant of righteousness - when in reality you have been pulled away from your sincere devotion to Christ and are unwittingly serving Satan. I know that's strong, but it can happen. Do not accept the devil's lie that you can't get out! It may be very costly financially, and a big blow to your pride, but you must come clean, renounce the shameful ways, and fully return to Christ. I shudder to think what awaits you in the future if you don't.

We certainly do not need witch hunts in the church. We do not want to get paranoid, imagining that every other person is serving the devil. The message of the wheat and tares is very relevant here: *while you are pulling the weeds, you may uproot the wheat with them.* Untold damage has been done to the church by well-meaning people who tried to pull out the weeds.

The best way to challenge the false gospels and false apostles is to carefully preach the Word of God, live it out, and encourage and practice a sincere devotion to Jesus. The danger is magnified with the internet, where there is so little oversight of what is available. Protect yourself by being part of a church with a godly pastor who preaches the Bible.

Examine the fruit, pray, and do not get complacent. More than ever we need the fullness of the Holy Spirit and the spiritual gift of discerning of spirits.

A fearful judgment and eternal punishment awaits those who do not repent of their deceit, and continue in the masquerade. Frankly, I think it will be worse for them than for those involved in what we consider blatant sins, or even those in other religions. These "angels of light" are bold enough to come into God's temple and masquerade as servants of righteousness.

Don't get lost in the masquerade.

Chapter 21 Real Boasting
2 Corinthians 11:16-33

¹⁶ I repeat: Let no one take me for a fool. But if you do, then tolerate me just as you would a fool, so that I may do a little boasting. ¹⁷ In this self-confident boasting I am not talking as the Lord would, but as a fool. ¹⁸ Since many are boasting in the way the world does, I too will boast. ¹⁹ You gladly put up with fools since you are so wise! ²⁰ In fact, you even put up with anyone who enslaves you or exploits you or takes advantage of you or puts on airs or slaps you in the face. ²¹ To my shame I admit that we were too weak for that!

Spiritual abuse

Tragically, people can be so deceived they willingly submit to spiritual abuse. The false teachers in Corinth:

- Enslaved the Corinthian church (AMP: *"assume control of your souls"*; GNT: *"order you around"*).
- Exploited them (AMP: *"devour [your substance, spend your money"*]; NLT: *"take everything you have"*). It's the same word Jesus used in Luke 20:47 when he denounced the Pharisees because they "devoured" widows' houses.
- Took advantage of them (AMP: *"prey upon or deceive you"*; NLT: *"take control of everything"*).
- Put on airs, exalted themselves (AMP: *"are arrogant"*).

- Slapped them in the face. This was a sign of great disrespect, as Jesus was slapped in the face by those who arrested him. Whether physically or emotionally, the false apostles were abusive.

Paul is amazed that the church actually put up with these abuses – and may even have welcomed them! But such is the nature of spiritual deception. Unfortunately, these abuses are all too common today. Many innocent, sincere people, who think they are serving God, get caught up in these schemes. Beware of any ministry that stoops to such tactics! That controlling, arrogant spirit is from the evil one, even if he is often disguised as an angel of light.

Paul's boast

Since the Corinthians will not listen to godly counsel and common sense, Paul is forced to descend to their level and talk foolishness. But while he might talk foolishly, he is no fool. In 1 Corinthians 2:13 Paul wrote about words taught by the Spirit: *"This is what we speak, not in words taught us by human wisdom but in words taught by the Spirit, expressing spiritual truths in spiritual words."* The Corinthians should be convicted of their lack of spiritual discernment. *"The man without the Spirit does not accept the things that come from the Spirit of God, for they are foolishness to him, and he cannot understand them, because they are spiritually discerned."* (1 Corinthians 2:14) Since spiritual talk is foolishness to them, Paul is forced to talk their nonsense, instead of Spirit-taught words.

Chapter 21 Real Boasting

²¹Whatever anyone else dares to boast about—I am speaking as a fool—I also dare to boast about. ²² Are they Hebrews? So am I. Are they Israelites? So am I. Are they Abraham's descendants? So am I. ²³ Are they servants of Christ? (I am out of my mind to talk like this.) I am more. I have worked much harder, been in prison more frequently, been flogged more severely, and been exposed to death again and again. ²⁴ Five times I received from the Jews the forty lashes minus one. ²⁵ Three times I was beaten with rods, once I was pelted with stones, three times I was shipwrecked, I spent a night and a day in the open sea, ²⁶ I have been constantly on the move. I have been in danger from rivers, in danger from bandits, in danger from my fellow Jews, in danger from Gentiles; in danger in the city, in danger in the country, in danger at sea; and in danger from false believers. ²⁷ I have labored and toiled and have often gone without sleep; I have known hunger and thirst and have often gone without food; I have been cold and naked. ²⁸ Besides everything else, I face daily the pressure of my concern for all the churches. ²⁹ Who is weak, and I do not feel weak? Who is led into sin, and I do not inwardly burn? ³⁰ If I must boast, I will boast of the things that show my weakness.

What would you appeal to if you were challenged as Paul was? What do most apostles or Christian leaders point to?

- The many churches planted?
- The great healings performed?
- The number of people saved?
- The attendance at major crusades?
- The impressive internet site?

- Graduating *Summa Cum Laude* from one of the best seminaries in the country?
- The number of best-selling books published?
- The cable/satellite systems worldwide that air their daily TV program?

Paul is ready to challenge these imposters, and he has an impressive record.

The false apostles almost certainly were Jewish. They may have implied that Paul was not a real Jew since he identified so much with the Gentiles, so Paul starts by leveling the field. He is every bit as Jewish as they are:

- He is a Hebrew
- He is an Israelite
- He is a descendent of Abraham

He did not bother mentioning his outstanding pedigree as a Pharisee trained under Gamaliel (Acts 5:34, 22:3), which would put him far above any of them. His reason for that will soon become apparent.

Are they servants of Christ? Paul is out of his mind to even suggest they are, since he just said (vv. 13-15) that they are serving the devil. But even if they were serving Christ, they certainly could not surpass Paul's experience:

- He worked harder
- Was imprisoned more frequently
- Was flogged more severely
- Repeatedly had been close to death
- Been hungry and thirsty

- Been cold and naked
- Fasted more and longer
- Gone without sleep
- Been constantly on the move (perhaps to avoid some of these hardships)

Exactly how he quantified his work, floggings, imprisonments, or fastings as being greater than these false apostles is unclear, but chances are they had never even known imprisonment or flogging. In case the false apostles made light of these dangers, Paul gets more specific. He says he was:

- Whipped five different times with 39 lashes from the Jews
- Beaten with rods three times (scourging that often ended in death)
- Stoned (with rocks, not drugs)
- Shipwrecked three times – including spending a night and day on the open sea
- In danger in the city, country, at sea, and on rivers – in other words, everywhere!
- In danger from Jews, Gentiles, bandits, and false believers – in other words, everyone!

Not only are there false apostles, but also false believers. There is an unknown number of them in our churches posing a real danger to the true servants of Christ.

That is horrific enough in itself, but this was even harder for Paul to bear:

- He was responsible before God for all the churches he founded, and felt that burden daily
- When someone was weak and struggling, Paul actually felt it
- When someone was sinning, he inwardly burned with indignation

Without God's help, that would be an impossible burden to bear!

If this is "boasting," Paul was not very good at it! He rebuked the false apostles by boasting about his own suffering! To him that was a much more valid sign of authenticity than external success. Yet Paul rarely went around trumpeting his sufferings or complaining about them. Suffering was simply part of being an apostle. While the false apostles may have experienced some of these problems, they were probably more like the hireling Jesus describes in John 10, who abandons the sheep when things get rough. The false apostles almost certainly did not feel the burden Paul had for the personal well-being of the believers. How do apostles and church leaders today measure up against Paul's experience?

What about you?

- Have you thought you had it rough?
- Would you be able to put up with all that Paul experienced?
- Are you ready to throw in the towel now, with the relatively light pressures you are facing?

- If you are in leadership, do you feel the burden Paul did for your people? It's normal if you do! You should!
- Do you get close enough to really empathize with them and feel their pain?

³¹ The God and Father of the Lord Jesus, who is to be praised forever, knows that I am not lying. ³² In Damascus the governor under King Aretas had the city of the Damascenes guarded in order to arrest me. ³³ But I was lowered in a basket from a window in the wall and slipped through his hands.

Perhaps Paul's experiences sound so unbelievable that he feels the need to make this assertion of their veracity. The reference to the Damascus experience seems out of place, but his opponents may have pointed to it as an act of cowardice: sneaking out of town in a basket instead of facing his accusers. Since he was not present in Corinth, they may have implied that he was cowardly avoiding a face-to-face confrontation with them.

By his foolishness, Paul has shown just how shallow his opponents are. They were caught up in power, money, and appearances, but had no knowledge of the suffering Savior Paul served so faithfully. It would only be a matter of time before that became apparent in Corinth, but in the meantime great harm could be done to the church, and that was what Paul wanted to avoid.

Chapter 22 Strength in Weakness
2 Corinthians 12:1-10

¹I must go on boasting. Although there is nothing to be gained, I will go on to visions and revelations from the Lord. ² I know a man in Christ who fourteen years ago was caught up to the third heaven. Whether it was in the body or out of the body I do not know—God knows. ³ And I know that this man—whether in the body or apart from the body I do not know, but God knows— ⁴ was caught up to paradise and heard inexpressible things, things that no one is permitted to tell. ⁵ I will boast about a man like that, but I will not boast about myself, except about my weaknesses. ⁶ Even if I should choose to boast, I would not be a fool, because I would be speaking the truth. But I refrain, so no one will think more of me than is warranted by what I do or say, ⁷ or because of these surpassingly great revelations.

In defending his apostleship, Paul has already taught that suffering and weakness validate God's call more than great accomplishments. If he is so humble, it seems surprising that he would even mention these amazing revelations. Yet the battle with the false apostles is so fierce that he feels obligated to draw on all the ammunition he can possibly summon. The false apostles probably talked extensively about their own "revelations" and supernatural experiences, which impressed the gullible Corinthians. But those experiences were hard to verify. Be careful what you believe! Do not base your opinions of leaders and their ministries – or your personal decisions - on their self-reported angelic visitations, visions, or other assorted supernatural manifestations. There is nothing wrong with them, but there is good reason to be suspicious of someone who focuses on them. Paul refers to them only in the context of this extraordinary situation.

We learn some interesting things about Paul's special encounters with the Lord:

- This great apostle apparently had only one such experience, and that was 14 years ago. It is highly unlikely someone is going to have regular revelations of this magnitude. It was about 20 years since his Damascus road experience, so this revelation was probably during his so-called "silent years" in Syria or Cilicia (the time between his Damascus road vision in 35 AD and the Council of Jerusalem in 49 AD).
- Paul leaves open the possibility of a man being physically caught up to heaven, but it may be impossible to know whether it was bodily or in a vision. Indeed, it does not even seem clear to Paul!
- There is a definite place Paul calls "paradise" (a word which usually means "garden" or "park'). It is a place you can visit, where we can expect to spend eternity. There is a lot of talk about visits to heaven or hell today. Some are probably valid. Such experiences – like Paul's - affirm our belief in heaven.
- Oh, to know what some of those inexpressible things were, and why no one is permitted to talk

- about them! Think about the great things we will learn when we get to heaven!
- Paul refers to "third heaven," the only time it is mentioned in the New Testament. In Paul's time people may have considered our sky the first heaven, outer space second heaven, and God's dwelling place third heaven.
- An experience like Paul's is obviously life-changing! The great danger for anyone with special visitations is conceit. Watch for it in those who claim such experiences, and in yourself, should you be so privileged. Far from giving them a super-spiritual trouble-free life, they come with a price and great responsibility.

Have you ever had a vision? Joel's prophecy (Joel 2:28) as quoted by Peter at Pentecost indicates visions would be a common part of the Spirit-filled experience. In some parts of the world they are. While we certainly do not want to overemphasize them, we should be open to visions and special spiritual experiences.

[7] Therefore, in order to keep me from becoming conceited, I was given a thorn in my flesh, a messenger of Satan, to torment me. [8] Three times I pleaded with the Lord to take it away from me. [9] But he said to me, "My grace is sufficient for you, for my power is made perfect in weakness." Therefore I will boast all the more gladly about my weaknesses, so that Christ's power may rest on me. [10] That is why, for Christ's sake, I delight in weaknesses, in insults, in hardships, in persecutions, in difficulties. For when I am weak, then I am strong.

The nature of thorns in the flesh:

- They are the gift nobody wants. Since they come from outside you and are given to you, they don't necessarily indicate a natural weakness, sin, or failure. Have you been down on yourself – or others – because you thought a thorn reflected those things?
- They are given for a purpose. They keep our eyes on God and remind us of our human frailty. God undoubtedly uses them many ways. In Paul's case it was to keep him humble, and that may be typical. What do you think is the purpose of the thorn(s) in your life?
- Thorns will not kill you, but they won't go away, either. They are a constant annoyance. "In the flesh" may mean a bodily affliction, or it might refer to the carnal, sinful nature we all struggle with.
- At least in Paul's case, the thorn was a messenger from Satan. You can rebuke Satan and cast him out all you want, but apparently God allows Satan's messengers to afflict even his choicest servants! "Messenger" is the same word used for "angel." Paul is likely saying his thorn was a demon. Not possession, but an annoying evil spirit that God allowed to accomplish his purposes. Perhaps if the same end can be achieved by gentler means we can avoid the satanic messenger.
- Like any demon, the thorn torments you. I find it almost shocking that God would actually arrange for the torment of one of the greatest Christians who

ever lived! Are you in torment? Have you tried everything you can to get free from it? Have you even been tempted to turn away from the Lord because he hasn't delivered you? Or leave a marriage or ministry because of it? Or, in the extreme, kill yourself? Can you deal with the possibility that you might be tormented for the rest of your life?

Many guesses have been made about the nature of Paul's thorn: problems with his eyesight, a physical affliction that made him unattractive, or a chronic illness (perhaps epilepsy). Yet Paul must have been physically strong to endure all he did through the years! Other possibilities mentioned have been depression, the people (maybe the Jews) who constantly bothered him, some sexual temptation, or even same-sex attraction. From the way he describes it, and to merit being torment from Satan himself, I think we can assume it was more than just bad eyesight.

What is your thorn?

You might not have any. That could mean you cooperate with the Lord and don't need that kind of reminder, or it could mean your impact for Christ is so insignificant at this point that there is no need to distract you from ministry. Most of us likely have some thorn we struggle with. What is yours? Take some time and write down all the possible thorns. Pray about them and reflect on whether they fit the profile of a thorn. Your perspective on some of your struggles may change!

Does a thorn in their flesh betray weak faith?

I have pleaded far more than three times for thorns to be removed from my life! My guess is that you have too! Perhaps Paul was used to getting prayers answered the first time, so to ask three times was highly unusual! Jesus asked three times in Gethsemane to avoid the suffering of the cross, but was also told no. Jesus' attitude was as ours should be: not my will, but yours be done. It's not a lack of faith to include that in your prayers! We cannot order God around!

Is your faith weak if you have to ask more than once? I have heard teachings that you should ask only once and then give thanks for the answer. But that seems to contradict what Paul did here. Others have questioned whether we even need to ask, since God already knows our needs (Matthew 6:8). Jesus taught about persistence in prayer. James said you do not have because you do not ask (James 4:2). There is nothing wrong with sharing what's on your heart with God. Be open, however, to hearing "no," as Jesus and Paul did, and then trust that God has a good reason for it.

God's grace is sufficient!

If God answered all our prayers, giving us health and everything else the world says we need, we wouldn't need God! We have become incredibly spoiled! Life on this earth is far from perfect, and Christ never guaranteed us paradise now! That is why Paul needed that surpassingly great revelation to get a glimpse of paradise! In the meantime we are forced to rely on God's grace. If you are tempted to rely on yourself, God may allow circumstances that force you to

Chapter 22 Strength in Weakness

rely on him. People like Paul, who are naturally gifted, may find it harder to let go of self. Our weaknesses reveal Christ's sufficiency. Real faith is not so much about claiming your healing and everything else you want, as it is about trusting that indeed God's grace is enough.

Whatever you are facing, God's grace is sufficient for you! What is exposing your weakness right now? What prayers have gone unanswered? What opportunities do those unanswered prayers provide for God to glorify himself and show his great power? Does your trial make you look less like a victorious Christian? Even a failure? That was exactly what the false apostles were claiming about Paul! And that claim is what Paul was rejecting! It's not about you! It's about God and his grace!

Strength in weakness

Christianity cannot be an invention. Nobody would create a faith that glories in weakness! What is alarming is that perhaps the majority of Christians do not glory in weakness! We want strong faith, strong marriages, and strength to tackle whatever confronts us. We resort to power plays in the church, with the government, and in relationships with other faith communities.

The false apostles in Corinth gloried in their power and impressive spiritual strength. In challenging them, Paul has completely changed the playing field. Paul glories in his weakness, because he has learned that the weaker he is, the more Christ can manifest his power. It totally transformed Paul's attitude toward difficulties in this life. Like James in the first chapter of his letter (James 1:2), we can rejoice in trials. Insults don't touch us. Hardship is an opportunity for God to provide and help us. Persecution helps us identify with our Savior and reminds us that we are not of this world. Difficulties allow God to show his wisdom and power. Instead of bemoaning these things, we are to understand that they are part of this life, and allowed by God so his power can be demonstrated. That means you can relax! You don't have to have it all together! Difficulties do not mean you're less of a man or woman! Hardship does not mean you didn't work enough! Those false apostles looked like they had it all together. You may look longingly at others in your church or on the job who seem so capable. Whatever they have they may have achieved in their own strength. If so, as impressive as they may be, their achievements ultimately won't change lives and probably won't last. As Charles Hodge wrote: "When emptied of ourselves we are filled with God."

I know it's radical to glory in weakness. If you can make the shift to glory in your own weakness, you will begin to see God's power like never before. Paul says he gloried in his weakness for Christ's sake. Is it about you, or Jesus? Do you want him to be lifted up and glorified? Do you want people drawn to him – or to you? It may be hard, but try rejoicing in your weaknesses this week! And watch out for those thorns!

Chapter 23 True Apostolic Ministry
2 Corinthians 12:11-21

^{11} I have made a fool of myself, but you drove me to it. I ought to have been commended by you, for I am not in the least inferior to the "super-apostles," even though I am nothing. ^{12} I persevered in demonstrating among you the marks of a true apostle, including signs, wonders and miracles. ^{13} How were you inferior to the other churches, except that I was never a burden to you? Forgive me this wrong!

True apostolic ministry is marked by signs, wonders, and miracles

Do you want to know if someone is truly an apostle? Paul explicitly states that a true apostle will be marked, among other things, by signs, wonders and miracles. Whether the "super-apostles" demonstrated these signs is unclear, but supernatural events were plentiful in Paul's ministry. Are they evident in the ministry of "apostles" you know? If not, their claim to apostleship may need to be examined.

We have repeatedly seen how uncomfortable Paul has been when forced to defend his apostleship. It was so twisted – they should have been commending him as an apostle! Somehow his refusal to accept money from them was pivotal in their doubts about him. If he was a real apostle, why didn't he act like the other "super-apostles" who so eagerly took their money?

¹⁴ Now I am ready to visit you for the third time, and I will not be a burden to you, because what I want is not your possessions but you. After all, children should not have to save up for their parents, but parents for their children. ¹⁵ So I will very gladly spend for you everything I have and expend myself as well.

The true apostle gladly gives of himself for the individuals in his care

Accepting their money would have been one simple way to settle the issue, but that would violate some fundamental principles of true apostolic ministry which guided Paul. Every ministry should follow them!

- **I will not be a burden to you.** The one ministering should never be a burden to those receiving the ministry.
- **I want you – not your possessions.** Have you ever been in a church where you felt nobody was really interested in you as a person? They wanted you for what you could do for the church, for your tithe, or for some agenda. Focus on the person! Let that person know you are truly interested in them as an individual – and not what you can get from them! Too often people who do not seem to serve the leaders' agenda get discarded!
- **Children should not have to save for their parents, but parents for their children.** Many parents save for their children's education, help them purchase their first house, or try to have a generous inheritance to pass on to them. Here Paul is

speaking in the framework of spiritual children and parents. A spiritual father should be ready to give all he can to support those in his care! Apostles should never get rich off their spiritual children!

- **The spiritual father should have an attitude of self-sacrifice.** Like a loving natural father who will do anything for his children, there should be a willingness to totally expend himself financially, emotionally, and spiritually. A good shepherd lays down his life for the sheep (John 10:11). The children should not be expected to expend themselves on behalf of the parent. Ministry is about giving and pouring out your life, not about what you can get.

I like the way John Calvin paraphrased Paul: "I am in quest of a larger hire than you think of. I am not contented with your wealth, but I seek to have you wholly, that I may present a sacrifice to the Lord of the fruits of my ministry."

[15] If I love you more, will you love me less? [16] Be that as it may, I have not been a burden to you. Yet, crafty fellow that I am, I caught you by trickery! [17] Did I exploit you through any of the men I sent to you? [18] I urged Titus to go to you and I sent our brother with him. Titus did not exploit you, did he? Did we not walk in the same footsteps by the same Spirit?

A true apostle walks by the same Spirit and in the same footsteps as his coworkers

For the third time Paul reminds the Corinthians that he hasn't been a burden! That would be unloving – and his ministry is all about love. What he does long for is their love in return. The men Paul sent followed these same principles, never exploiting the church.

What a beautiful picture of the unity we should have when we minister with others: all walking in the same footsteps! It can only happen when we are all led and filled by the same Spirit. There should be consistency among all team members. The leader must be aware of how his representatives are operating and respond accordingly if anything is out of order.

^{19} Have you been thinking all along that we have been defending ourselves to you? We have been speaking in the sight of God as those in Christ; and everything we do, dear friends, is for your strengthening. ^{20} For I am afraid that when I come I may not find you as I want you to be, and you may not find me as you want me to be. I fear that there may be discord, jealousy, fits of rage, selfish ambition, slander, gossip, arrogance and disorder. ^{21} I am afraid that when I come again my God will humble me before you, and I will be grieved over many who have sinned earlier and have not repented of the impurity, sexual sin and debauchery in which they have indulged.

Everything a true apostle does is for the strengthening of the church

It hasn't been all about Paul! The Corinthians may not think so, but Paul's purpose in writing this letter was to enable him to continue ministering to them, and thus strengthen the church. Yet Paul still has fears about his upcoming visit. Does that surprise you?

When you anticipate a ministry trip - or anything that involves stepping out in faith - do you ever have fears? Are you able to name them? Is it wrong to have those fears? Paul shares four specific fears he has about his upcoming visit:

- There could be disappointment and misunderstanding between him and the Corinthians. They may not live up to his expectations, and he may not measure up to theirs. "Will they accept me? Will things be awkward when I get there?" It's normal to have some insecurity when venturing into a difficult situation – even for a great man of faith.
- There may be discord, jealousy, fits of rage, selfish ambition, slander, gossip, arrogance and disorder. From what Paul knows about this church, these things are very possible. Nobody wants to step into this kind of situation! What similar fears do you have as you approach your church? Your home? Paul did not simply declare that these things would not be there. He was a realist, and knew that - despite his prayers - the situation could be tense. You might think these tensions should not have affected him – but he did not simply dismiss the fear.
- God will humble Paul, perhaps because of the sin present in a church he has labored so hard for and bragged about to others. That might seem to confirm the judaizers' assertions that gentiles couldn't be true Christians.

- Paul would find unrepented sin. If the instructions given in 1 Corinthians have not been followed he will be grieved by the continued sin.

As Paul ends his letter, a great deal of uncertainty remains about a highly valued relationship. He could still lose this church! Although he didn't state it as a fear, the fear of failure, fear of losing your spouse or family, or fear of losing your ministry, often underlies other fears. Paul certainly could not be faulted for not trying to win the Corinthians back! We also do our best to maintain those relationships, but ultimately we must leave them in the Lord's hands.

How does your ministry compare with the signs of true apostolic ministry? What fears are you facing right now regarding your church, your work, or your family? Are you able to express them, and perhaps even share them with the people who are causing them?

Chapter 24 Examine Yourself
2 Corinthians 13:1-6

[1] This will be my third visit to you. "Every matter must be established by the testimony of two or three witnesses." [2] I already gave you a warning when I was with you the second time. I now repeat it while absent: On my return I will not spare those who sinned earlier or any of the others, [3] since you are demanding proof that Christ is speaking through me. He is not weak in dealing with you, but is powerful among you. [4] For to be sure, he was crucified in weakness, yet he lives by God's power. Likewise, we are weak in him, yet by God's power we will live with him in our dealing with you.

As Paul neared the end of his letter, he was still fighting for the soul of this church.

He wanted to impress on the Corinthians how serious he was about addressing their sin. Despite what his enemies might say, Paul was not making idle threats. He would do whatever was necessary to restore purity and godly order. He put special weight on this third visit, the third "testimony" which will confirm his judgment of the church. Almost like the umpire's "Three strikes and you're out," this visit will be pivotal.

Christ has given us the awesome privilege and responsibility of being his mouthpiece. If you claim to speak for him, make sure it really is his word! And carefully evaluate others who claim to speak for him! Great harm has been done to individuals and the church by falsehoods spoken in the name of Christ. Both Paul and the false apostles claimed to be speaking for Christ. The Corinthians put the burden on Paul to prove he was speaking the truth - proof he was confident would be provided by the demonstration of Christ's power and authority during his visit.

The Corinthian church did not operate apart from apostolic authority. There is no hint they might just "leave the denomination and go independent," nor claim that they alone had the right to deal with problems in their church. The nature of the authority God has established in the church demands a covering over local congregations. The New Testament simply does not give room for a totally independent, self-governing church. The many examples of abuses in such churches demonstrate the need for that godly authority. At the same time, this letter points to the very real possibility of false apostles exploiting that authority.

Those false apostles accused Paul of being weak. The believer, however, has a very different understanding of power and weakness than the world. Many feel it is weak to rely on God – to have a "crutch." Willingly giving up your life and crucifying your flesh may seem weak. Christ's crucifixion was the ultimate expression of weakness, yet that humiliating act released amazing supernatural power. Even after walking with Christ for years you may be very aware of your human weakness, but the knowledge of that weakness enables you to live by God's power. Those who rely on themselves know nothing more than their own strength. It truly is not about you! Instead, it's about you getting out of the way so God's power can be displayed!

The Corinthians were obsessed with power: Supernatural manifestations in their services, impressive apostles who seemed to have great spiritual power, and demonstrations of the Spirit's power in their daily lives. To them, any weakness indicated a lack of faith, and Paul seemed weak. Even Christ was suspect for his supposed weakness and humility. Why didn't he stand up to the Pharisees and Jewish leaders? Why didn't he call down fire, or angels? The Corinthians had embraced a distorted gospel, leading Paul to make a surprising request:

⁵ Examine yourselves to see whether you are in the faith; test yourselves. Do you not realize that Christ Jesus is in you—unless, of course, you fail the test? (JBP: You should be looking at yourselves to make sure that you are really Christ's. It is yourselves that you should be testing, not me. You ought to know by this time that Christ is in you, unless you are not real Christians at all.)

⁶ And I trust that you will discover that we have not failed the test.

The Corinthians had the nerve to demand that Paul prove himself, but he turned it around, saying *they're* the ones who have something to prove! Are they truly saved? Paul was not so sure. He had put himself to the same test – and was confident he and his companions would pass.

In this call to self-examination it's easy to overlook God's amazing provision for true believers: Christ lives in us. Are you aware of that in your daily life? Is there any evidence of Christ living in you? If he is, there should definitely be some.

When was the last time you did this self-examination, or challenged your church to examine themselves? Are you afraid to, in case you might not pass the test? Do you assume just because someone is a long-time church member they are "in the faith?" Paul did not make such an assumption. Based on his experience with the Corinthians and their acceptance of "apostles" whom he called servants of Satan, he probably feared many were not really saved.

How can you be sure you really are in the faith? A book could be written answering that question, but here are a few tests:

- **The fruit.**
    - *Every good tree bears good fruit, but a bad tree bears bad fruit. A good tree cannot bear bad fruit, and a bad tree cannot bear good fruit. Every tree that does not bear good fruit is cut down and thrown into the fire. Thus, by their fruit you will recognize them* (Matthew 7:17-20).
    - *The seed that fell among the thorns represents those who hear God's word, but all too quickly the message is crowded out by the worries of this life and the lure of wealth, so no fruit is produced* (Matthew 13:22).
- **Brokenness over sin and increasing freedom from besetting sin.** Numerous passages speak of

habitual, unrepented sins that betray a lack of saving faith:
- *Do you not know that wrongdoers will not inherit the kingdom of God? Do not be deceived: Neither the sexually immoral nor idolaters nor adulterers nor men who have sex with men nor thieves nor the greedy nor drunkards nor slanderers nor swindlers will inherit the kingdom of God* (I Corinthians 6:9-10).
- *The acts of the flesh are obvious: sexual immorality, impurity and debauchery; idolatry and witchcraft; hatred, discord, jealousy, fits of rage, selfish ambition, dissensions, factions and envy; drunkenness, orgies, and the like. I warn you, as I did before, that those who live like this will not inherit the kingdom of God* (Galatians 5:19-21).
- *Those who belong to Christ Jesus have crucified the flesh with its passions and desires* (Galatians 5:24).

- **What occupies your time, affection, and thoughts.**
    - *Those who live according to the flesh have their minds set on what the flesh desires; but those who live in accordance with the Spirit have their minds set on what the Spirit desires. The mind governed by the flesh is death, but the mind governed by the Spirit is life and peace* (Romans 8:5-6).

- **The inner confirmation of the Holy Spirit.**
  - *The Spirit you received brought about your adoption to sonship. And by him we cry, "Abba, Father." The Spirit himself testifies with our spirit that we are God's children* (Romans 8:15-16).
- **Evidence of the Spirit's presence in your life.**
  - *If anyone does not have the Spirit of Christ, they do not belong to Christ* (Romans 8:9).
  - There should be fruit of the Spirit (*love, joy, peace, forbearance, kindness, goodness, faithfulness, gentleness and self-control*, Galatians 5:22-23) and manifestations of the Spirit in gifts of service.
- **Public confession of faith in Christ and solid belief in what he accomplished on the cross.**
  - *To all who receive him, to those who believe in his name, he gives the right to become children of God* (John 1:12).
  - *If you declare with your mouth, "Jesus is Lord," and believe in your heart that God raised him from the dead, you will be saved. For it is with your heart that you believe and are justified, and it is with your mouth that you profess your faith and are saved* (Romans 10:9-10).
  - There should be a willingness to speak to others about your faith.
- **Doing God's will; obedience.**
  - *"Not everyone who says to me, 'Lord, Lord,' will enter the kingdom of heaven, but only*

Chapter 24 Examine Yourself

> *the one who does the will of my Father who is in heaven. Many will say to me on that day, 'Lord, Lord, did we not prophesy in your name and in your name drive out demons and in your name perform many miracles?' Then I will tell them plainly, 'I never knew you. Away from me, you evildoers!'"*
> (Matthew 7:21-23)

If you have failed this test, don't despair! I have met many pastors and long-time church members who realize they were never saved! The purpose of a test is to point out what you need to learn, what to study, and how to prepare yourself for the final exam. Far better to find out now, than when you are standing before God on judgment day! The church has been plagued by "easy believism" and "cheap grace" which offers a ticket to heaven with no cost or true surrender to Christ's Lordship.

May God's Holy Spirit guide you and open your eyes as you honestly examine yourself. If you pass the test, rejoice in God's grace and salvation! If you fail, Jesus is waiting right now to receive you and give you a new life!

Chapter 25 What is Truly Important
2 Corinthians 13:7-14

⁷ Now we pray to God that you will not do anything wrong— not so that people will see that we have stood the test but so that you will do what is right even though we may seem to have failed. ⁸ For we cannot do anything against the truth, but only for the truth. ⁹ We are glad whenever we are weak but you are strong; and our prayer is that you may be fully restored.

Paul's purpose in urging a self-examination is not that he would look good as the great apostle who had raised up a strong church. He was truly concerned about them and their relationship with the Lord. Be careful about how much you depend on others to feed your ego! Some subtle signs that you may doing that:

- Are you more concerned about your church growing in Christ so they experience his fullness, or so people applaud the great anointing on your ministry? You may be thinking about the books and TV appearances that are sure to follow.
- Do you get upset when your kids are in sin because you long for them to have a solid relationship with Christ – or because their sins will make you look bad as their parent?

Even at the risk of looking weak, dedicate yourself to whatever will truly benefit those God has entrusted to you, whether it be your family or your church.

[10]{} This is why I write these things when I am absent, that when I come I may not have to be harsh in my use of authority—the authority the Lord gave me for building you up, not for tearing you down.

Husband, God has given you authority in your home, not for tearing down your wife and kids, but for building them up. Pastor, God has given you that authority in your church.

Authority is given, not seized – and it is given for a purpose. Some people are harsh in their use of authority. Are you? Why? There appear to be times when it may be justified, but it is too easy for authority to go to men's heads and become a power trip. If you are not in a proper relationship with God, you will not have his authority. Many lack his authority resort to asserting themselves in the flesh. There is, however, nothing to back them up. If you are in a place where God has given you authority – your home, your church, your job – you can be sure God is standing with you as you use it for the well-being of those entrusted to you. (For a much deeper study of authority see my book *Made to Reign: Using (and Losing) Your Kingly Authority*.)

[11]{} Finally, brothers and sisters, rejoice! Strive for full restoration, encourage one another, be of one mind, live in peace. And [then] the God of love and peace will be with you.

Paul leaves us with several commands, mostly dealing with relationships in the Body.

Chapter 25 What is Truly Important

1. **Rejoice!** No matter what is going on in your life, keep the joy of the Lord! You may not be able to rejoice *because* of your circumstances, but you can still rejoice *in* them. Is there something stealing your joy right now?
2. **Strive for full restoration.** (AMP: *Be strengthened, perfected, completed, made what you ought to be*) Could you say you are striving to be all you can be? Are there areas in your life that need restoration? Areas where you are weak? Even immature? What can you do about that?
3. **Encourage one another.** (AMP: *be encouraged and consoled and comforted*) We all want to be encouraged – but do you realize there are people all around you who need encouragement? How about your husband or wife? Your mother or father? Your children? Coworkers? Who could you encourage today? Many of us aren't very good at encouraging others. Give some thought to how you can be an encouragement.
4. **Be of one mind.** The importance of church unity is seen over and over in the New Testament. If Satan can divide us, he can destroy us. Start at home! A house divided against itself cannot stand (Matthew 12)! Are you of one mind with your spouse? Are you known as a peacemaker who fosters unity? Or do you tend to create conflict? Is there someone you need to speak to about restoring your relationship? Are you willing to humble yourself and give up your insistence that you are always right, so you can be

of one mind - even if you don't necessarily agree with them?
5. **Live in peace.** Shalom — that total state of well-being, at peace with self, others, and God — was so important to the Jews. Would you say you know peace in your life? In your home? When was the last time you did? What happened to that peace? What can you do to get it back? Could asking forgiveness be a first step? How can you keep your peace if you are in a church, home, or job where peace seems to be totally lacking?

As we do these things to foster relationships with others we experience more of God's love and peace. Fellowship should result in a deepened relationship with God. It is hard to know God's love and peace if there is disunity, discord, and discouragement in the Body.

^{12} Greet one another with a holy kiss. ^{13} All God's people here send their greetings.

Warm fellowship should exist among believers — in a local body, but also among all the churches. There should be regular communication with believers around the world. Today that is incredibly easy thanks to the internet. Who could you encourage by sending a greeting? How could you express a little more warmth (it doesn't have to be a kiss!) when you greet people in your church, letting them know you really care about them and are happy to see them?

^{14} May the grace of the Lord Jesus Christ, and the love of God, and the fellowship of the Holy Spirit be with you all.

Chapter 25 What is Truly Important

Who says the Trinity is not in the New Testament? Maybe that word is not used, but we see undeniable references to three distinct persons, with no suggestion that one is divine while the others are not. In the face of rising Islam and supposedly Christian sects that deny the Trinity, stand firm for what the Bible teaches about the Godhead, even though it may be difficult to understand!

Despite Paul's issues with this church, in closing he shares his longing for them to fully experience each member of this Trinity. Far more than a theological doctrine, the three persons give us an amazing opportunity to relate to God on three different levels:

- He is Lord and Master, but Jesus is also an older brother, your great high priest who intercedes for you and understands your human weakness from first-hand experience. He's in a perfect position to pour out unmerited favor, or grace, into your life. Are you still trying to make it on your own strength? Are you willing to give up your striving and start living in the grace Jesus longs to give you? Of course you don't deserve it – but you can never be good enough to earn it. You are not under the Law anymore! Enjoy your freedom and a deep relationship with Christ. He wants it even more than you do.
- The Father, who so loved you that he gave his only Son to purchase your salvation, loves you with that deep father-heart love. As a father, there are times when he is stern and may discipline you, but love is behind it all. Are you so busy about your life that you

hardly have time to spend with your Father? Could you use a little more love in your life? Have you been let down by others you thought loved you? His love is unchanging, unconditional, and unlimited.
- And then, most intimate of all, dwelling within you, is the Spirit. The counselor, comforter, and teacher. You are never alone! You can spend the whole day in fellowship with the Holy Spirit! Do you think the Spirit ever gets lonely inside you? Do you spend hours – even days? – acting as though the Spirit wasn't there? Do you realize the Spirit longs for fellowship even more than you do? How is your fellowship with the Spirit? What can you do to improve it?

Conclusion

Here we are at the end of a book so full of rich teaching. How amazing that it is often overlooked! Some of the key verses remind us of what we've studied:

Praise be to the God and Father of our Lord Jesus Christ, the Father of compassion and the God of all comfort, who comforts us in all our troubles, so that we can comfort those in any trouble with the comfort we ourselves receive from God. For just as we share abundantly in the sufferings of Christ, so also our comfort abounds through Christ. (1:3-5)

We were under great pressure, far beyond our ability to endure, so that we despaired of life itself. Indeed, we felt we had received the sentence of death. But this happened that we might not rely on ourselves but on God, who raises the dead. (1:8-9)

But thanks be to God, who always leads us as captives in Christ's triumphal procession and uses us to spread the aroma of the knowledge of him everywhere. For we are to God the pleasing aroma of Christ among those who are being saved and those who are perishing. (2:14-15)

Not that we are competent in ourselves to claim anything for ourselves, but our competence comes from God. He has made us competent as ministers of a new covenant—not of the letter but of the Spirit; for the letter kills, but the Spirit gives life. (3:5-6)

Now the Lord is the Spirit, and where the Spirit of the Lord is, there is freedom. And we all, who with unveiled faces contemplate the Lord's glory, are being transformed into his image with ever-increasing glory, which comes from the Lord, who is the Spirit. (3:17-18)

And even if our gospel is veiled, it is veiled to those who are perishing. The god of this age has blinded the minds of unbelievers, so that they cannot see the light of the gospel that displays the glory of Christ, who is the image of God. (4:3-4)

But we have this treasure in jars of clay to show that this all-surpassing power is from God and not from us. We are hard pressed on every side, but not crushed; perplexed, but not in despair; persecuted, but not abandoned; struck down, but not destroyed. We always carry around in our body the death of Jesus, so that the life of Jesus may also be revealed in our body. (4:7-10)

Therefore we do not lose heart. Though outwardly we are wasting away, yet inwardly we are being renewed day by day. For our light and momentary troubles are achieving for us an eternal glory that far outweighs them all. So we fix our eyes not on what is seen, but on what is unseen, since what is seen is temporary, but what is unseen is eternal. (4:16-18)

For Christ's love compels us, because we are convinced that one died for all, and therefore all died. And he died for all, that those who live should no longer live for themselves but for him who died for them and was raised again. (5:14-15)

Therefore, if anyone is in Christ, the new creation has come: The old has gone, the new is here! (5:17)

We are therefore Christ's ambassadors, as though God were making his appeal through us. We implore you on Christ's behalf: Be reconciled to God. God made him who had no sin to be sin for us, so that in him we might become the righteousness of God. (5:20-21)

Do not be yoked together with unbelievers. For what do righteousness and wickedness have in common? Or what fellowship can light have with darkness? (6:14)

Remember this: Whoever sows sparingly will also reap sparingly, and whoever sows generously will also reap generously. Each of you should give what you have decided in your heart to give, not reluctantly or under compulsion, for God loves a cheerful giver. And God is able to bless you abundantly, so that in all things at all times, having all that you need, you will abound in every good work. (9:6-8)

For though we live in the world, we do not wage war as the world does. The weapons we fight with are not the weapons of the world. On the contrary, they have divine power to demolish strongholds. We demolish arguments and every pretension that sets itself up against the knowledge of God, and we take captive every thought to make it obedient to Christ. (10:3-5)

Therefore, in order to keep me from becoming conceited, I was given a thorn in my flesh, a messenger of Satan, to torment me. Three times I pleaded with the Lord to take it away from me. But he said to me, "My grace is sufficient for you, for my power is made perfect in weakness." Therefore I will boast all the more gladly about my weaknesses, so that Christ's power may rest on me. That is why, for Christ's sake, I delight in weaknesses, in insults, in hardships, in persecutions, in difficulties. For when I am weak, then I am strong. (12:7-10)

Is there any particular verse or passage that God has particularly quickened to you?

Are there any ways he has challenged you?

As you reflect back on the book, can you think of at least one thing he is specifically calling you to do?

Appendix: A Biblical Understanding of Comfort

What is comfort?

Comfort is far more than a pat on the back and saying everything will be alright. Webster defines it as "giving strength and hope; cheering, or easing someone's grief or trouble." Our word comes from the Latin, meaning *to strengthen greatly*. But the original Greek text uses three words, which have a much fuller meaning. The English translations used in the New International Version give us a sense of that meaning. The numbers in parentheses indicate how many times that translation is used:

parakleo: Urge (26 times), encourage (25), begged (12), pleaded with (7), comforted (6)

paraklesis: Encouragement (15), comfort (11), appeal (2)

parakletos: Counselor or advocate (4), one who speaks in another's defense

Paraklesis involves calling someone to your side. You may be familiar with *parakletos*, the word used for the Comforter, the Holy Spirit, the One called alongside to help you. A *parakletos* could also be a counsel for the defense in court; an advocate. Biblically, comfort is being there for someone; entering into their pain, and walking with them through a difficult time. Comfort gives strength, whether or not it involves words.

How does God comfort us?

His rod and staff: *Even though I walk through the darkest valley, I will fear no evil, for you are with me; your rod and your staff, they comfort me* (Psalm 23:4).

His promises: *My comfort in my suffering is this: Your promise preserves my life* (Psalm 119:50).

His Word: *I remember, Lord, your ancient laws, and I find comfort in them* (Psalm 119:52).

> *But the one who prophesies speaks to people for their strengthening, encouraging and comfort* (1 Corinthians 14:3).

His love: *May your unfailing love be my comfort, according to your promise to your servant* (Psalm 119:76).

His Spirit: *And I will ask the Father, and he will give you another advocate (counselor, comforter) to help you and be with you forever— the Spirit of truth* (John 14:16-17).

God uses us to bring comfort, often by simply being present:

Isaac brought her into the tent of his mother Sarah, and he married Rebekah. So she became his wife, and he loved her; and Isaac was comforted after his mother's death (Genesis 24:67).

Comfort, comfort my people,
 says your God.

Speak tenderly to Jerusalem,
  and proclaim to her
that her hard service has been completed,
  that her sin has been paid for,
that she has received from the Lord's hand
  double for all her sins (Isaiah 40:1-2).

For when we came into Macedonia, we had no rest, but we were harassed at every turn—conflicts on the outside, fears within. But God, who comforts the downcast, comforted us by the coming of Titus, and not only by his coming but also by the comfort you had given him. He told us about your longing for me, your deep sorrow, your ardent concern for me, so that my joy was greater than ever (2 Corinthians 7:5-7).

Jesus, who is called Justus, also sends greetings. These are the only Jews among my co-workers for the kingdom of God, and they have proved a comfort to me (Colossians 4:11).

Comfort is part of the mission Jesus claimed as his own:

The Spirit of the Sovereign Lord is on me,
  because the Lord has anointed me…
to comfort all who mourn,
  and provide for those who grieve in Zion—
to bestow on them a crown of beauty
  instead of ashes,
the oil of joy
  instead of mourning,
and a garment of praise
  instead of a spirit of despair.
(Isaiah 61:1-3)

We can resist and refuse the comfort available to us:

Then Jacob tore his clothes, put on sackcloth and mourned for his son many days. All his sons and daughters came to comfort him, but he refused to be comforted. "No," he said, "I will continue to mourn until I join my son in the grave." So his father wept for him (Genesis 37:34-35).

When I was in distress, I sought the Lord;
   at night I stretched out untiring hands,
   and I would not be (refused to be) comforted (Psalm 77:2).

This is what the Lord says: "A voice is heard in Ramah, mourning and great weeping, Rachel weeping for her children and refusing to be comforted, because they are no more" (Jeremiah 31:15).

Comfort can seem to elude us:

When Job's three friends, Eliphaz the Temanite, Bildad the Shuhite and Zophar the Naamathite, heard about all the troubles that had come upon him, they set out from their homes and met together by agreement to go and sympathize with him and comfort him (Job 2:11).

"I have heard many things like these; you are miserable comforters, all of you!" (Job 16:2).

My eyes fail, looking for your promise; I say, "When will you comfort me?" (Psalm 119:82).

"Both high and low will die in this land. They will not be buried or mourned, and no one will cut themselves or shave their head for the dead. No one will offer food to comfort those who mourn for the dead—not even for a father or a

mother—nor will anyone give them a drink to console them (Jeremiah 16:6-8).

The idols speak deceitfully, diviners see visions that lie; they tell dreams that are false, they give comfort in vain. Therefore the people wander like sheep oppressed for lack of a shepherd (Zechariah 10:2).

God has a special place in his heart for those who mourn and suffer, promising them comfort.

Some who find comfort in worldly things will not find comfort in the future:

Blessed are those who mourn, for they will be comforted (Matthew 5:4).

"But woe to you who are rich, for you have already received your comfort" (Luke 6:24).

"But Abraham replied, 'Son, remember that in your lifetime you received your good things, while Lazarus received bad things, but now he is comforted here and you are in agony.'" (Luke 16:25).

www.ingramcontent.com/pod-product-compliance
Lightning Source LLC
Chambersburg PA
CBHW071459040426
42444CB00008B/1413